Lawrence Dallaglio has won everything the game has to offer, including the Rugby World Cup in 2003, a hat-trick of consecutive Premiership titles and two Heineken Cups with Wasps. He captained his country and is regarded as one of the world's greatest ever back-row forwards. He won eighty-five caps for England and three Lions caps. Dallaglio retired from professional rugby in 2008. He is married with three children and lives in Richmond, London.

David Trick, who worked with Lawrence putting together these stories, was a keen athlete whilst at school winning the National Schools 100m Championship. However, he couldn't better his time of 10.4 seconds and this coupled with the incredibly boring conversations about diet and training sessions led him to rugby. He spent twelve enjoyable seasons with Bath in the eighties and early nineties and played for England at every level from Under-16 to the full team, making his debut in 1983. His main reason for choosing rugby was the opportunity to go 'on tour' every year or so.

LAWRENCE DALLAGLIO

MORE BLOOD, SWEAT AND BEERS

with David Trick

SIMON & SCHUSTER

London · New York · Sydney · Toronto · New Delhi

A CBS COMPANY

First published in Great Britain as 'World Cup Rugby Tales' by
Simon & Schuster UK Ltd, 2011
This edition published in Great Britain by Simon & Schuster UK Ltd, 2012
A CBS COMPANY

1 3 5 7 9 10 8 6 4 2

Simon & Schuster UK Ltd
1st Floor
222 Gray's Inn Road
London WC1X 8HB

www.simonandschuster.co.uk

Simon & Schuster Australia, Sydney
Simon & Schuster India, New Delhi

A CIP catalogue record for this book is available
from the British Library

ISBN 978-0-85720-347-2

Typeset by M Rules
Printed and bound by CPI Group (UK) Ltd, Croydon CR0 4YY

To all the rugby players up and down the country, the old and the young, the fast and the slow, those who relish the mud and the rain and those who would rather be in the bar.

Without you the game would not exist.

Contents

Foreword

Wooden Spoon

I am delighted this book will help to benefit Wooden Spoon and in turn the children the charity supports. Founded in 1983, Spoon has its roots firmly set in the sport of rugby. It was conceived on 19 March 1983 in Dublin, after England lost their final encounter in the Five Nations Championship, which meant that having successfully failed to win any of the previous three matches in the campaign they picked up the mythical Wooden Spoon of sport. Peter Scott (Life Honorary President) and his son Mike, together with three friends, witnessed the English demise that day and were presented with a memento of the occasion by some very caring Irish acquaintances. An actual wooden spoon.

The story goes like this. On the flight back to Heathrow one of the five highlighted what a fantastic weekend they'd all had, irrespective of the result, and how sad it was that there were some children who didn't even get the chance to play sport, let alone international sport. So it was decided to hold a golf day at Farnham Golf Club with the express aim of raising some money and making a donation to the Variety Club Sunshine Coach appeal. They also intended to present their wooden spoon to the losing team. The golf day took place in September and raised an incredible £8,000, far more than had been anticipated. A decision was made to donate the majority of the money to the Variety Club as planned, but also to retain a small amount and form a new charity to help disadvantaged children. The Wooden Spoon Society as it was called back in the eighties was up and running. In the end it was decided not to hand over the actual wooden spoon but to keep it within the charity, where it remains to this day, a symbol of where it all began.

The growth of Wooden Spoon has been phenomenal. In the twenty-eight years since its formation the charity has raised somewhere in the region of £18 million, at a current rate of around £1.5 million per year.

The mission statement of the charity is simple: Wooden Spoon exists to improve the quality and prospect of life for children and young people who are disadvantaged physically, mentally or socially.

It strives to achieve this through the delivery of a combination of capital projects and social programmes. Capital projects have included medical treatment and recovery centres, sports and activity areas, sensory rooms and gardens, playgrounds and hydrotherapy pools. In 2009 Wooden Spoon introduced the Spoon Community Rugby programme. Since then, Spoon has invested over £800,000 in SCR projects to help 31,000 disadvantaged young people across the UK and Ireland find inspiration, motivation and opportunities to achieve and succeed. Initial research has highlighted the amazing benefit of this particular initiative and it goes from strength to strength.

Currently there are over forty regional volunteer committees as well as a central national team, and the charity proudly boasts more than 10,000 members across the UK and Ireland. The regional committees undertake local fundraising activities and ensure the money raised is spent on projects in their respective communities, which means that the benefit of fundraising is always immediate, visible and lasting.

The vast majority of money is raised via events and challenges, ranging from sporting dinners and golf days – the annual four-day golf trip to La Manga each May is the highlight of the year for the majority of participants! – through to the Four Peaks Challenge, when teams of four climb the highest peaks in Scotland, England, Wales and Ireland within forty-eight hours, and the John O'Groats to Land's End cycle ride over a seven-day period, which always proves popular with those taking part.

I have been involved with Wooden Spoon for many years and am proud to be the Honorary President of the Middlesex Region. I wish the charity and the children they support all the very best in the years to come.

Lawrence Dallaglio, OBE
June 2011

Introduction

One-offs

In 2009 during a 'quiet' night out with a few mates from the world of rugby it occurred to me we'd all enjoyed so many experiences, both on and off the field of play, that it would be a great idea to share some of them with a wider rugby audience. Often a good idea remains just that, but for some reason this particular one stayed with me for several days. I contacted a few of the usual suspects – Jerry Guscott, Jason Leonard, Michael Lynagh etc. – and ran the concept past them. Once I'd explained what the word 'concept' meant, they all agreed it was an excellent idea, particularly as the majority of the rugby fraternity see a match on a Saturday and read a few reports in the press but have little idea what actually goes on behind the scenes.

Having made the decision to produce a book I started to contact players from around the world asking them to contribute. I sent an email to approximately 100 players past and present, requesting their favourite story (circa 1,000 words). What could be easier? And that was even allowing for the front-row forwards, who would clearly take some time considering which were their favourite stories and even more time typing the words. I honestly thought I would have the 100,000 words necessary to satisfy the editor and publisher within a few weeks.

Having sent out the requests I sat back and waited for the vast array of stories to start filling my inbox. I allowed a few days for consideration, a couple more for the writing process, and then started to check my emails several times an hour, anticipating the arrival of the literary gems, no doubt humorous, probably unbelievable, and hopefully tales I hadn't heard before. After a couple of weeks I had received one written response (huge thanks to the former England and British Lions winger David Duckham MBE). Encouragingly, I had also received about twenty replies from players saying they thought the book was a good idea and would be sending their contributions in the near future.

Eight weeks after my initial contact with my rugby 'mates' I had in my possession three stories, one of which was less than seventy-five words in length! Around thirty of the boys had replied saying they were more than happy to supply a story but in all honesty could not be 'arsed' to write one, so would I be good enough to give them a ring so they could tell me the tale. A further 50 per cent didn't bother to respond (thanks, lads). In amongst this pretty dismal effort was a great text from the aforementioned England team-mate of many years Jerry Guscott, saying quite simply, 'Happy to help, when someone has written a story for me, email so I can approve it, cheers.' Further proof (if it were needed) that Jerry was happy for someone else to do all the work and he would graciously take all the praise – a mirror of his playing days in my opinion.

Having sold the idea to a publisher who was as enthusiastic as me, it became obvious I was going to have to do a lot of the writing, which was certainly not part of the original plan, so I enlisted help from two good friends, former Wasps team-mate Damian Hopley (now Chief Executive Officer of the Rugby Players Association) and the former Bath and England winger David Trick. Between the three of us we listened to a variety of tales, tapped away on our laptops for hour after hour and ultimately hit the deadline – not, I hasten to add, the first deadline the publisher requested, or indeed the second, but we definitely hit one of them, as the book *Lawrence Dallaglio's Rugby Tales* was published and in the shops by late October.

I remain very proud of the book; however, given the amount of work that went into it, I do remember saying in December 2009 at a celebratory lunch with all those concerned with its production, 'Job done – NEVER AGAIN.'

Sir Steve Redgrave once famously said immediately after winning his 1996 Olympic gold medal, 'If anyone sees me going anywhere near a boat again they have my permission to shoot me.' Admittedly his statement was rather more high-profile than mine, made as it was in a small London restaurant to about seven people, but the result was the same. We both took time to reflect and reached the conclusion that perhaps it was worth giving it another go. Steve went on to further golden glory in the Sydney Olympics of 2000, while the simple fact you are holding this book means I have also done it again.

I can only speculate on why Steve changed his mind, but my reason was simple. Since the book was published, countless people have told me how much they enjoyed it. Some read it from cover to cover in one sitting and others dipped into it from time to time. The vast majority of stories were true and gave the reader an insight into some of the amazing antics players throughout the generations have got up to during matches, on tours or in bars around the globe. In addition to the enjoyment it gave to so many people, it also provided a decent financial contribution to the Rugby Players Association Benevolent Fund.

This time around I will be making a contribution to the charity Wooden Spoon. Many players, indeed contributors to this book, have an active involvement with Wooden Spoon and the various fundraising activities they undertake every year. In my Foreword I have explained in some detail how the charity works but for those of you who may not yet have read that section, Wooden Spoon is the charity of British and Irish Rugby supporting mentally, physically and socially disadvantaged children. They believe all children and young people deserve the chance to live happy, fulfilled lives regardless of the challenges they may face. Spoon harnesses the spirit and values of rugby to give these youngsters throughout the UK and Ireland a chance to achieve their full potential in life. Hopefully you will have great enjoyment reading this book while sharing in the knowledge that you (or the person who bought the book) are also helping a very worthy charitable cause at the same time.

Having been through the process once, I was much better equipped this time to deal with the highs and lows of collecting the stories. David Trick once again agreed to assist me and between us we have contacted World Cup participants, listened to their stories and knocked them into some kind of shape. At least this time I had a bit more experience and didn't waste time writing quite as many stories which due to legal reasons never saw the light of day. You are a lucky boy, Jason Leonard.

I'll be taking a look at the six Rugby World Cups to date, three of which I watched and three I participated in (should have been four, but I won't get into that just yet), giving my personal memories of each before letting loose some of the greats of the game with their own tales of debauchery, heroism (well, maybe not) and much else besides. To avoid any confusion while you are enjoying reading the stories, I should explain that where the contributions cover more than one tournament, I've tried to locate them in the section I felt was most relevant.

Before we get stuck in, however, by way of some background I thought it would be useful (and perhaps even interesting) to run through the history of the RWC, hopefully demonstrating how the tournament has evolved from a hastily arranged competition in 1987 to the global event it has become watched by a television audience in excess of 4 billion people.

RWC – A Brief History

Like all good tales, the story of the Rugby World Cup begins a long, long time ago . . . on 8 December 1870 to be precise, when a letter appeared in the *Scotsman* newspaper and *Bell's Life,* a London magazine, inviting footballers from England and Scotland to participate in a match played by the 'Rugby Rules'. North of the border the date of Monday 27 March 1871 was set, and preparations were made for the match to take place in Edinburgh. Academical Cricket Club was approached to lease their ground and Raeburn Place was therefore credited as hosting rugby's first ever international match between Scotland and England.

One hundred and sixteen years later, in 1987, the inaugural Rugby World Cup took place, kicking off on 22 May with a group match between New Zealand and Italy (70–6) at Eden Park, Auckland and ending at the same venue on 20 June with New Zealand defeating France 29–9 to become the first holders of the Webb Ellis Cup.

In a country where rugby is often regarded as a religion, hosting and winning the first Rugby World Cup was definitely very important for New Zealand. For much of the twentieth century the All Blacks had been regarded as one of the best teams in international rugby, but without a World Cup such claims were impossible to prove. The fact that New Zealand has not won the four-yearly competition since 1987 has arguably made the victory even more important to All Black fans. Photographs of their captain David Kirk holding the Webb Ellis Cup in triumph are among the most famous sporting images in New Zealand.

What is less well known is how the first Rugby World Cup came about. This fascinating story highlights a number of key themes, including the struggle between the amateur ideal and creeping professionalism, tensions between the British home unions and southern hemisphere countries, and international protests over sporting contacts with South Africa.

Rugby union has been a medal sport at the modern Summer Olympic Games, being played at four of the first seven competitions. The sport made its debut at the 1900 Paris games where the gold medal was won by the host nation. It subsequently featured at the London games in 1908, the Antwerp games in 1920 and finally at the Paris games in 1924. The United States is the most successful nation in Olympic rugby tournaments, having won the gold medal in both 1920 and 1924, and with the sport being dropped by the International Olympic Committee shortly after Paris, the USA held the title of unofficial world champions for over sixty years.

In the mid-twentieth century nearly every major sport,

and many minor ones, launched world championships. Even those with a regular place in the Olympics found such an event profitable both in financial and public relations terms. World Cups began for football in 1930, for rugby league in 1954, for men's field hockey in 1971 and for cricket (limited-overs) in 1975; even handball had a world championships in 1938 and orienteering in 1966. Yet as late as into the eighties, the International Rugby Football Board (IRFB) refused to even think about a World Cup, the concern being that such a tournament would inevitably bring money into the game, with unknown consequences.

The fact that rugby's professional rival, rugby league, now had a World Cup was another reason the IRFB opposed the idea. In the sixties the former Australian international Harold Tolhurst and Manly club stalwart Jockey Kelaher suggested finding a world champion by holding a month-long tournament in Australia, with Great Britain, France, South Africa and New Zealand to fight it out with the home side. The IRFB was not amused and refused to sanction it in any way. Even competitions to find national club or regional champions were seen as contrary to the spirit of the game. Until 1968, when South Africa's Currie Cup became an annual event, only France among the rugby powers held a national championship. New Zealand launched its provincial championship in 1976, but clubs in Britain still played only 'friendlies'.

By the early eighties winds of change were threatening to blow down the house of cards of amateur rugby. The debacle of the 1981 rebel Springbok tour of New Zealand, which saw widespread protests against the South African team and the apartheid regime, together with the success of New Zealand's footballing All Whites in qualifying for the 1982 FIFA World Cup and the continuing loss of Australia's top rugby union players to rugby league, were all signs of the vulnerability of the sport even in its southern hemisphere strongholds. In response, the Australian and New Zealand unions made separate proposals to the IRFB for a Rugby World Cup.

Forced to do something, the IRFB asked Australia and New Zealand to come up with a feasibility study. With 1987 the only southern winter free of major sports events for the rest of the decade, there was no time to waste. If a World Cup was not approved at the IRFB's March 1985 meeting, the concept would once again go on the back burner for years.

Each of the eight full members of the IRFB – Australia, New Zealand, South Africa, England, Ireland, Scotland, Wales and France – had two votes, so the four home unions would all but have a veto if they stuck together.

South Africa was the great unknown. The sports boycott made it impossible for the country to play abroad. As always, South African Rugby Board president Danie Craven (an IRFB delegate) thought ahead. He realised that favours granted at no real cost now might well pay dividends later. His decision to support the proposal in effect guaranteed that South Africa would later host a similar tournament – if the first one succeeded and apartheid was relaxed. The wily former Springbok captain thus set the stage for the 1995 World Cup (won, of course, by South Africa at home), which cemented the place of rugby, until then a symbol of Afrikaner supremacy, in the multicultural nation.

This left France as the power broker. French Rugby President Albert Ferrasse decided to vote for a World Cup provided non-IRFB countries were included. D-Day was 21 March 1985, the venue the headquarters of the French national railway. The delegates were whisked by TGV to a lunchtime cruise on the Rhône. After intense lobbying, the vote was taken back in Paris. Delegates from England and Wales broke ranks with the naysayers and the proposal was passed by a margin of 10–6. A Rugby World Cup would be held in 1987. A body with no paid staff, or even any money to call its own, had just two years to organise rugby's first global tournament.

The Rugby World Cup was set to take place in May or June 1987, early in the southern winter but not too long after the completion of Europe's Five Nations. The organising committee was headed by John Kendall-Carpenter, the Englishman who had voted in favour of the competition in 1985. With South Africa out of the international scene, nine non-IRFB nations would be needed to fill the four four-team pools. Some choices were obvious: Italy, Romania and Argentina all had respectable recent records against the major teams. Canada, USA, Japan, Fiji and Tonga also had a long history of playing the game, and the first three offered lucrative television markets. Minnows Zimbabwe were granted the last place to give southern Africa an interest in the event.

The IRFB spent a year arguing over the distribution of profits, which were yet to be made. Knowing they had the old guard over a barrel, the host unions held out for the best terms they could get. The deal reached in March 1986 gave Australia and New Zealand all their net gate receipts. They would also share 48 per cent of the income generated by the tournament representatives (the commercial company managing the event). The other unions taking part would share most of the rest. Also agreed at the meeting was the appointment of British sports marketing company West Nally as the tournament representatives. They trumped rival bidders by offering US$5 million upfront for the rights. The Australian insistence on payment in advance was to prove wise – West Nally failed to survive the October 1987 stock market crash.

Potential sponsors demanded stadiums that were 'clean' (free of all other advertising). Because of this and Australian rugby politics, the traditional New South Wales Test venue, the Sydney Cricket Ground, was unavailable. Auckland's Eden Park would host the final, and both semi-finals would be played in Australia. Brisbane's Ballymore Oval could readily stage one. The Sydney semi-final was allocated to the small Concord Oval, which the New South Wales Rugby Union was developing as its base. With rugby weak outside these two cities, only one pool would be played in Australia. Eight venues in New Zealand would host the other three pools.

Sponsors were not secured until shortly before the

tournament kicked off. When they were announced, the wisdom of including Japan and the United States was confirmed. KDD, a Japanese telecommunications company, was the main sponsor. The others were Mazda, Rank Xerox and New Zealand Breweries. Commercialism was suddenly everywhere. The name of a beer, Steinlager, was even painted on the small buckets in which sand was carried out to place-kickers. Despite a stern circular from the New Zealand Rugby Football Union (NZRFU), this ruse was repeated in the final. In rugby's brave new world, even official sponsors were not above a little guerrilla marketing.

The host television rights were shared by public broadcasters, the Australian Broadcasting Corporation and Television New Zealand. At the last minute, the BBC decided to pay £1 million to cover the tournament. This fee looked excessive, but by the 1991 World Cup it would seem the bargain of the century.

On the whole the tournament witnessed fairly one-sided matches, the seven IRB members proving too strong for the other teams. Half of the twenty-four matches across the four pools saw one team score forty or more points. Even still, 600,000 spectators came out to watch (an average of 18,900 per match) in addition to a worldwide television audience of 300 million from 17 different countries. With regard to the commercial success, it generated £3.3 million in income with a surplus of somewhere in the region of £1 million.

Throughout the hasty preparation for 1987, it was considered by the IRB to be a 'one-off'. (How could they think that? Mind you it does remind me of something . . . oh yes, the first *Rugby Tales*!) No plans were made for future tournaments until the tournament was over. I suspect now, however, they are pretty pleased with themselves that they decided to give it another go. Evidence of the phenomenal growth of the Rugby World Cup can be demonstrated by the fact that in the space of twenty years the RWC has become the third-largest sporting event in the world, behind only the football equivalent and the Olympics. That's pretty impressive.

Before I leave this brief historical run-through, there is one other snippet I'd like to share, something I've only found out about recently. It concerns the World Cup whistle.

It seems that the first game of every World Cup to date has been started by the same whistle. The whistle is over 100 years old and bears an inscription saying it was used by Gil Evans in the Test match between New Zealand and England in December 1905, a match the All Blacks won 15–0.

This piece of rugby history is also believed to have been used by Albert E. Freethy in the final of the 1924 Olympics in Paris when the United States beat hosts France 17–13 at the Colombes Stadium.

A year later Freethy blew the whistle to dismiss Cyril Brownlie in the Test between New Zealand and England at Twickenham in January 1925, making him the first player to be sent off in an international match.

The whistle has been housed in the New Zealand Rugby Museum in Palmerston North since 16 April 1969 when they held their inaugural function, having been donated by Stan Dean, who for many years was the chairman of the NZRFU and manager of the 1924/25 All Blacks.

There, now you know.

Bedroom Farce

Enough history. It is time we got on to the stories, but just before we do, I'd like to say a big thank you to all the guys who have contributed World Cup tales and memories for this book. I am indebted to you all. As I hear a story occasionally it triggers a memory of my own about a particular incident. I was out with some fellow knackered old rugby players last night, telling a few lies about how great we used to be and generally reminiscing about the good old days when our bodies were stronger. During the evening I was reminded of a story which occurred during the 2007 World Cup. This morning, it made me chuckle again so I thought I would write the 'short and sweet' tale and include it here, as a taster of things to come.

With the 2007 tournament being hosted by France it was relatively easy for the friends and families of players to make the short trip over the Channel and meet up from time to time. Whilst it's vital for the squad to concentrate on the task in hand, it's also important to get a break from the continuous training, analysis and general preparation that take place during a World Cup campaign. To spend time with friends and loved ones provides welcome relief from the monotony of the rugby bubble in which players are required to live.

It was noticeable how many of the players' wives and girlfriends seemed keen to visit their men when we were staying in the Trianon Palace Hotel in Versailles (now a Waldorf Astoria hotel). Situated about a dozen miles from the heart of Paris and set within magnificent woodlands, it has been described as one of France's finest luxury retreats, complete with a magnificent spa and an exquisite French restaurant. A far cry from the Marseille Holiday Inn we were to stay in a week later, but I will say more about that later in the book. It is way too early to inflict that story on you just now.

One late arrival was Mike Catt's wife Ali (yes, she really is called Ali and if you think about it for a second it's clear she must have been very much in love with Mike to agree to marry him). Having reached the hotel, Ali was keen to catch up with several of the other partners and decided it was more important for her to go out on the town with them rather than wait for her husband to finish training. The group disappeared into the night and by all accounts had a splendid evening, sampling the local cuisine and drinking as much French wine as they could manage.

Arriving back at the hotel fully refreshed, the girls entered the lift and pressed level 3, the floor occupied by the majority of the players. It was at this point Ali realised she had no idea which was her husband's room. So she walked along the corridor hoping there might be a sign or familiar smell to help locate Mike's room. About halfway along one of the doors was open and inside she spotted a kitbag with the initials MC. With huge relief, she entered the empty room and collapsed into bed.

I have no idea who was the most shocked fifteen minutes later when Martin Corry entered his room to find Mike Catt's wife fast asleep in his bed. *Ooh là là,* as they say in France. I think.

Right, this time I really am done wittering on. I shall now hand you over (after I've had my say, of course) to the wit and wisdom of rugby's finest. Good luck.

1987

I've already gone over the birth of the Rugby World Cup in my introduction, but in case you skipped that (and who could blame you) I'll quickly go over again the set-up for this first step into the unknown.

Once the decision had been made to proceed it left little more than two years to lay the foundations of a tournament that would finally provide a method to establish a true world champion. The inaugural event was hosted predominantly by New Zealand with Australia acting as co-hosts.

Argentina were invited to take the place of South Africa – who were excluded from international rugby whilst the system of apartheid remained in place – with other invitations extended to Fiji, Tonga, Japan, Canada, Romania, Zimbabwe, Italy and the United States for the sixteen-team tournament to be held in May and June 1987.

The teams were split into four pools of four, three of which were based in New Zealand with the other, featuring

Australia, hosted in Sydney and Brisbane. The top two nations in each pool progressed to the quarter-finals.

New Zealand were the favourites to win the tournament and they definitely relished the opportunity to prove they were the dominant force in world rugby. Before the tournament started the All Blacks were told by their coach, Brian Lochore, they were playing for 100 years of New Zealand rugby-playing tradition, because they had been world champions (according to Brian, although it is hard to dispute, I suppose) without the trophy to prove it. No pressure there then.

The first match was between New Zealand and Italy and took place on 22 May at Eden Park, Auckland. Before the game the All Blacks performed the haka for the first time in a World Cup and with immaculate timing John Kirwan of New Zealand went on to grace this ground-breaking game by scoring one of the best tries ever seen at international level, running almost the entire length of the pitch beating several players in the process. The hosts won the game easily, 70–6, and the victory helped to unite the country which had been somewhat divided by the NZ Cavaliers' unofficial tour of South Africa in April 1986, breaking the international sporting embargo levied on the South Africans. It's fair to say there was a degree of apathy towards the tournament in the early stages, but as it progressed it began to capture the imagination of the home supporters and television viewers burning the midnight oil in the northern hemisphere.

Wales had a convincing 16–3 win over England in their quarter-final in Brisbane, while in New Zealand the All Blacks brushed aside Scotland. Australia and France secured the remaining two berths.

The semi-finals were in stark contrast to each other. Let's just say New Zealand beat Wales by 49–6 in a game even more one-sided than the score suggests. The other match proved to be very exciting, thanks largely to the fact that in true Gallic tradition France just kept attacking and attacking, throwing caution to the wind as they ran the ball at every opportunity. Australia came back at them with counter-attacks and eventually a wonderful try scored by the French legend Serge Blanco right in the corner of the pitch secured a thrilling 30–24 victory.

The All Blacks then won the final 29–9 at Eden Park and although France were well beaten, they had shown the southern hemisphere teams they were a major force in world rugby. As for New Zealand, it was a storybook finish confirming their status in the game. I'm sure no one could possibly believe they would not win at least one of the next five tournaments, but that, in my opinion (if not the opinion of New Zealanders), is the beauty of sport. It's often unpredictable and occasionally produces major upsets.

One person who is worthy of special mention, playing a key role in the development of rugby union on the world stage, is the late Vernon Pugh QC. Vernon was chairman of the International Rugby Board and Rugby World Cup Ltd. His energy and vision were instrumental in the expansion of the governing body to include ninety-four full members (increased from eight, quite a leap) and also in building the profile of the sport's showpiece event.

When you read some of the stories in the 1987 RWC section to follow I am sure you, like me, will be left with the impression that many of the players had no idea at all what to expect, and I'm reasonably confident their respective management teams had even less understanding of what was required. The All Blacks were the only team who prepared to win. The rest were there on tour, on holiday and in some cases just making up the numbers.

Regardless of the haphazard birth and the stuttering appreciation of most of the participating nations, the Rugby World Cup had arrived and the fun was just beginning.

Not in the Zone

When the 1987 Rugby World Cup took place I was fifteen years old and had an interest in the sport, but little more than that. It's fair to say the game was nowhere near as high on my list of priorities as it was to become in later years. One of the problems for me was the tournament took place on the other side of the world and at the time I was boarding at Ampleforth College. Nowadays the TV schedulers understand the huge interest shown by the northern hemisphere, which ensures that matches taking place in New Zealand or

Australia tend to kick off during the evening, local time, allowing European audiences to view them over breakfast.

Unfortunately they didn't have this foresight or knowledge back In 1987 so most of the matches were available to view at 3.00 a.m. in the UK. The chances of my housemaster allowing me to get up in the middle of the night to watch the games were less than zero. By 10.00 p.m. the dormitory doors were locked and bolted, chains securely in place, and it would have taken a fire for them to be opened before the following morning. In fact, anyone who has any knowledge of Ampleforth probably knows they operate in a different time zone from most of England, let alone other parts of the world. If it was 3.00 a.m. in New Zealand it would have been 1953 at Ampleforth. To be honest I'm still getting over the shock of being sent there.

As for the World Cup, from an English perspective it's probably just as well that I didn't catch much of the action. I don't recall us doing very well, and judging from the stories contributed by lads who participated, I'm not surprised. Organisation, discipline and dedication are three words (and I could mention many more) that didn't seem to feature on the radar of players or management in those early days. It would appear we got exactly what we deserved. That said, it's clear that a lot of fun was had as the northern hemisphere teams fell by the wayside.

Shiver Me Timbers

Gareth Chilcott

‘A firm favourite with the supporters during his playing days, Gareth Chilcott remains just as popular since retirement in his role as host of practically every overseas rugby trip organised by Gullivers Sports Travel in the last twenty years or so. I was fortunate to only play against him on a handful of occasions and I believe I have at least one scar (physical or mental) for every encounter. He was a hard man on the pitch and a gentleman off it. I remember an early game for Wasps against the mighty Bath side of that era. From the kick-off it became clear to me "Cooch" had little regard for the ball or indeed the opposition, he just wanted to impose his will and physical strength on anything dressed in black. As a callow youth of about nineteen years of age it seemed to

me that he succeeded on both fronts. John Reason, a superb rugby journalist, once wrote of Cooch, "He looked like a bit part actor playing the role of a Mafia assassin in search of his next victim." I'm not sure if this is complimentary or not, but having played against him I know exactly what John meant!

'Having spent many nights in his company, I can tell you he is one of the most entertaining characters to come out of the rugby world. It's no wonder he's still in great demand as an after dinner speaker. Just for the record his story below about being arrested is absolutely true. I won't give away here what it was actually for, but I for one am pleased he was released because a long-term period of incarceration would have been (deserved?) a sad loss to the sport of rugby.'

I admired Lawrence as a rugby player and have been even more impressed with his charitable work since retirement, in particular his Charitable Foundation which has raised millions of pounds for Cancer Research UK, Help for Heroes and the Rugby Players Association (RPA) Benevolent Fund amongst others. So when he gave me a ring regarding his World Cup book which is supporting a favourite charity of mine, Wooden Spoon, I was delighted to get involved.

If it's okay with the editor I want to contribute two stories: one concerns how I almost never made selection for a World Cup squad, or any other squad for that matter, and one relates to the inaugural World Cup in 1987, in which I played.

I'd had a great year in 1984: my club side Bath won the John Player Cup final at Twickenham for the first time and I made my international debut against Australia, also at Twickenham. To celebrate these events I accepted an invitation to help train the Thailand national rugby team for a few weeks during the summer. Little did I know I was going to be arrested for air piracy – yes, you've read that correctly – after the plane taking me to Bangkok made a forced landing in Karachi and four armed police deposited me in a local prison cell.

I was with a few mates from Bristol and we left Heathrow airport on Thai Air Flight 124. Shortly after take-off we landed in Paris to pick up a few more passengers, including the Agen rugby team who were departing for a tour of the Far East. This is when the seeds of disaster were sown. One or two of their lads spoke some English and we enjoyed a few beers together, every now and again breaking into song with a rendition of 'Rule Britannia' which was invariably followed by their version of the 'Marseillaise'. Perhaps inevitably, with alcohol levels rising, the Anglo–French rivalry began in earnest and, dare I say it, reached a boisterous level. We upheld the honour of the British for a creditable length of time as more and more glasses of plonk and beer were consumed by both parties. Unfortunately one of my mates, Martin Shepherd, who was particularly unsteady on his feet anyway, received a bit of a 'nudge' from the opposition, tripped over nothing in particular and fell, managing to split his head open on an armrest before hitting the floor. Out cold!

I was out of my seat and ready for action in an instant. Well,

I dragged myself up eventually at least. I managed to take out four of them with perfectly timed and expertly delivered punches without receiving a single blow in return, which was a hell of a lot easier than it sounds as they were strapped in their seats at the time and unable to move. I turned to face another Agen player running down the aisle and caught a blow to the side of the head. I knew it was going to be serious as I'd spotted a glass in his hand just before contact. We both looked at each other and then down at his hand which contained a crushed plastic cup. Let's just say I nodded in his direction and the job was done. The stewardesses were obviously not used to the slightly eccentric way in which the international camaraderie of rugby manifests itself, and one of them ran to the cockpit and convinced the pilot lives were at risk. He made an emergency landing in Karachi where uniformed police with rifles poured onto the plane, bashed my groggy mate Martin on the head with a rifle butt (he was only just coming around from the incident with the armrest) and slapped a set of handcuffs on me.

As we marched across the tarmac in the blazing sun another idiot idea came to me – make a run for it. With my hands handcuffed behind my back, I ran as fast as I possibly could, not thinking of the police and their weaponry. How I didn't get shot I'll never know. Of course there was nowhere to run and I soon found myself locked up in solitary for five days. From time to time someone would come into the cell and tell me I was departing on a flight later that day, but as each departure time came and went I began to get very worried. Eventually I was put on a flight to Bangkok, this time with my hands 'cuffed' at the front, and seated next to a striking couple and their beautiful young daughter. I had not shaved or showered for five days and wore the same set of clothes I'd been arrested in. Not a good look. The flight was full, so instead of moving as far away from me as possible, dad swapped seats with his daughter and acted as a human shield between me and his family.

Hours later, we landed at Bangkok and I was released from the handcuffs. Without a passport or luggage, which had arrived several days earlier on my original flight, I soon found myself a guest of the security forces once again. I tried to explain I was due to be coaching the national team and was a very important person. Twelve hours later my mate Andrew arrived with my passport and I knew I was just a few hours away from experiencing the Bangkok night life, or so I thought. No sooner had I arrived in our hotel, when my bowels gave out. I think I'd been fed something decidedly dodgy in Karachi. The net result was three days confined to my room, or more accurately the toilet.

To finish this story you need to know at the time there was very little rugby played in schools in Thailand, the majority of senior teams recruiting their playing personnel from the armed forces and universities. Such was my luck on this trip, Thailand had experienced horrendous monsoons and half the country was under water, with the result that the majority of the military players were out on flood relief, whilst the remainder contemplated wistfully where their pitches had once been before the rains washed them away. During a ten-week stint as coaching assistant, I spent six days in custody, two days in transit, three days on the toilet and managed just two training sessions, both of which took place with me standing in front of a blackboard. Rather than suggest I go home early, my hosts were apologetic about the weather and constantly checking I was okay. I genuinely wish I could have done more for them on the coaching front, but they provided me with enough memories to last a lifetime. I know, of course, that fighting on a plane is not a clever thing to do, but in my defence I was young, hot-headed, full of beer and red wine. I often think back on that episode now, and how easily I might have just disappeared from life languishing in a Karachi cell. I would never have experienced playing for England again, a British Lions tour, marriage and children. God knows I was lucky.

Beach Balls

Having survived my spell in the Karachi 'Hilton' I was going to make the most of freedom for the rest of my life, which obviously included the 1987 Rugby World Cup. A trip during which I improved my scuba diving, learnt the rules of water polo, reduced my golf handicap from 22 to 19, took my first sky dive, enjoyed my second ever bungee jump and frightened myself to death during a white water rapids trip in a relatively small inflatable boat. I also have a vague recollection of playing a bit of rugby.

The World Cup was a rugby tour with bells on, the only difference being you didn't know the date of your flight home until twenty-four hours prior to departure. I suspect I won't be the last to say so in these pages that the England approach was not all it could have been, especially when compared to the preparation of squads leading up to the more recent tournaments. Every single aspect is so totally different today; I look at the space-age kit provided for current international players and think about the bulky, baggy (although not that baggy in my case), heavy cotton shirts we used to play in, which more than doubled in weight if it rained. The only similarity is the red rose of England on the chest, which to me was always the most important thing.

One instance when England managed to get preparation spectacularly wrong was the period between qualification through the group stage and the quarter-final. Australia, Ireland, Wales and England were playing their quarter-final matches in Australia. Three of the four named countries travelled to Australia for training camps. The English management decided we needed some rest, recuperation and recreation to help recharge the batteries – a decision that was greeted with massive cheers from the squad, although with hindsight it was probably not what was required at such a critical stage of the tournament. So with the other teams heading into strict regimes we headed off to Hamilton Island, the leading resort destination in the Whitsunday Islands.

Four days of sunbathing, swimming and water polo would have been paradise at the end of a long season, not ideal for a match to determine who would proceed to the semi-final of the Rugby World Cup. During the break a decision was made to play a more expansive game, with Mike Harrison as England captain and right-wing obviously wanting to show the world what he and his fellow backs could do with the ball in their hands. Prior to this we had utilised the immense power of our forwards and dominated the opposition up front. I'm not certain the decision received unanimous support but when you're lying on a sun lounger with a Piña Colada in your hand, quite frankly it took too much effort to object.

The truth is England took a gamble which didn't pay off. Granted we felt fresh and relaxed when the quarter-final match started against Wales, but after a few minutes we all realised we would have done better if we'd done some proper training and worked on getting things right for the match. Our change of tactics failed miserably. We did release a great deal of ball to the backs but even though we had discussed it previously the arrival of that oval-shaped object still seemed to come as a surprise to them. We spent most of the game running backwards and cleaning up knock-ons and stray passes. We lost the match 16–3 with our only points coming from a solitary penalty from our full-back Jonathan Webb.

Twenty-four hours later we were on our way home, feeling disappointed we'd not progressed further in the tournament. Still, at least we were all sporting deep suntans and feeling completely stress-free.

Brought to Book

Gavin Hastings

'Gavin Hastings is a true legend of Scottish rugby and a former captain of the 1993 British and Irish Lions tour to New Zealand. For many years he appeared as a permanent fixture at full-back for Scotland, winning sixty-one caps, twenty as captain, as well as playing in all three Lions Tests in both New Zealand and Australia four years earlier. To achieve selection for a Lions Tour is the pinnacle of any British player's career; to gain selection for more than one is a true indication of the quality of player.

'During his career he set a new record for the most points scored in a major international. Just imagine what he would have achieved had he been born in one of the three big southern hemisphere rugby-playing nations. I first met Gavin prior to

embarking on my international career and was struck by how genuine and down to earth he was, a model player and a gentleman (at least in public).

'The following quote from Sir Ian McGeechan sums up Gavin as a player better than I ever could. "Gavin is a big man in every sense of the word, and his greatest asset was to engender confidence in those around him and to lead by example when the opposition had to be taken on. In New Zealand, they considered him simply the best full-back in the world."'

As a result of Scotland's membership of the International Rugby Board we were automatically selected to compete in the inaugural World Cup and looking back we probably arrived in New Zealand with high hopes and somewhat lower expectations. Obviously we were going to give it our best shot on the field of play but we were also not going to let the opportunity of several parties along the way slip through our fingers. On this front I like to think we were nothing short of ingenious.

We had hundreds of beautifully embossed gold invitations printed, complete with the Scottish Rugby Union logo. *'The Scotland World Cup Squad requests the pleasure of your company . . .'* with space left to fill in the time and venue by hand. Obviously the team's management, and indeed the grandees of the Scottish Rugby Union who were ostensibly the hosts, knew nothing of this enterprise. The highly impressive invitations were to be predominantly distributed by the boys who were not involved in the next match, commonly known as the 'dirt trackers'. At the time we were sponsored by Steinlager, a prominent New Zealand lager brand, ensuring the supply of alcohol was not a problem. We also had our prop forward Ian Milne (nickname 'The Bear' in light of his physical size and strength) on door duty, which was sure to deter undesirables from attempting to gain admittance.

The first extravaganza was scheduled to take place after our initial match in the group stage of the tournament, against France. Everything seemed to be in place and every contingency covered to ensure maximum pleasure. I say 'seemed' because we had overlooked one vital component – the nous, or lack thereof, of the dirt trackers. For some reason, not all of them had grasped the concept fully, as demonstrated by the surprisingly high number of blokes who turned up at that initial do. A meeting was hastily convened where it was made clear that our prestigious invites were to be handed out to 'beautiful young ladies' only. After all, these gatherings were ultimately for our benefit and not that of the guests.

From then on, our post-match shindigs were a huge success, which made it all the more surprising that we managed a few impressive performances on the pitch, the 20–20 draw with France perhaps best of all, which of course took place before the first party. At the end of the group stage we finished unbeaten in second place (on points difference) to the French, resulting in a quarter-final clash against the hosts and favourites New Zealand at Lancaster Park, Christchurch. Victory against the All Blacks was vitally important to the team. Obviously it would mean we progressed in the tournament, but in our eyes an even greater incentive was the fact that a win would ensure at least two more weeks on tour with a semi-final one week later which even if we lost would be followed by the third- and fourth-place playoff. If we were defeated by New Zealand we would be on a flight home the following day and as we still had a massive pile of invitations we were not keen to waste them. Simply put, more matches meant more parties.

Match day found us in the tunnel at Lancaster Park, side by side with the All Blacks, as our talismatic team-mate Finlay Calder walked up and down the Scottish line, urging us on. 'Come on, boys, we can do this, look at them, they're nothing, come on, this is ours,' etc., etc., etc. He was so sincere, everything he said genuinely heartfelt, that I along with the rest of the side believed at the very least we had a good chance of victory, even if it wasn't quite 'nailed on'. As impressed as we were with Finlay's passion, it did not seem to faze our opponents unduly. Indeed, one of their wingers, John Kirwan, very much a hero to millions of All Black fans, had clearly had enough of the ranting and tapped Finlay on the shoulder as he passed by. Finlay just glared as John produced a book from the pocket of his shorts and handed it to him.

'What the hell is this?' demanded Finlay, to which John calmly replied, 'It's a gift, something for you to read during your flight home tomorrow.' Finlay was furious. Had it been a cartoon, there would undoubtedly have been steam coming out of his ears. Before the incident could escalate (anyone who knows Finlay will understand this was more than a distinct possibility) the referee called both teams onto the pitch.

As the All Blacks performed the haka Finlay did not take his eyes off Kirwan and for the entire eighty minutes of the match it was obvious he was desperate to get his hands on him. For the record John was a big man blessed with a good turn of speed, unlike Finlay. To quote from *The Complete Book of Rugby*: 'Calder had the ability to use his drive, determination and innate knowledge of the game to overcome his undoubted shortcomings – in particular he was always a bit slow for an out-and-out open-side – this helped him become one of the most effective back-row operators of his generation.' Even with this drive, determination etc. he was still not capable of catching hold of John that day, which turned out to be the penultimate one of our campaign. We lost by 30–3, but at least I can proudly state that I scored all of Scotland's points in the match. It will come as no surprise that all the remaining invites were hastily distributed and Scotland left New Zealand with the impressive record of only having lost one match, to the eventual winners, and of hosting the biggest party Christchurch has ever witnessed.

Finlay may well have exhibited the pace of a lame elephant, but he also had the memory of one. A year later we were participating in a bicentennial celebration seven-a-side tournament in Sydney. Miraculously Scotland reached the final and 'only' had to beat New Zealand to lift the trophy. Halfway through the second half, with little between the two sides on the scoreboard, Kirwan made a break and for once in my life I managed to get hold of him and bring him down. As he was getting to his feet two things happened. First, John acknowledged my tackle with a knowing look, and second, out of the corner of my eye I saw Finlay frantically charging across the pitch, arms and legs all over the place. Moments later he absolutely clattered Kirwan who, having just got to his feet, was horizontal again within a fraction of a second. With the wind knocked out of him, John was briefly incapable of speech, and could only look up at Finlay proudly standing astride his body, ready for anything. It took a moment or two, but the big All Black did eventually regain some air, a degree of composure and his voice. 'That was f****** late, you Scottish twat.' With a wry smile Finlay replied, 'Aye, about twelve months too f****** late, you b******.'

In the Heart of the New Zealand Valleys

Ieuan Evans

'A genuine legend in Wales, Ieuan is generally regarded as one of the best Welsh wingers of all time, quite some accolade when you consider the country has produced the likes of Gerald Davies, J. J. Williams and John Bevan, to name but a few.

'He made his debut against France in 1987 and went on to gain seventy-two caps, twenty-eight as captain scoring thirty-three tries, at the time a Welsh record. He went on three tours with the British and Irish Lions, to Australia in 1989, New Zealand in 1993 and South Africa in 1997. His four tries in New Zealand made him the Lions' top try scorer. In his club career at Llanelli he won every domestic honour available, so in 1997, seeking new

challenges, he crossed the bridge to England and joined Bath. One year later he was part of the team which won the Heineken Cup, beating Brive 19–18 in the final. Deciding that was probably as good as it gets at club level he announced his retirement from the sport.

'He now runs his own marketing and communications company and has become an established broadcaster, often seen giving viewers his expert opinion during televised international matches.'

The Welsh team have never been as successful in World Cups as they were in the inaugural tournament in 1987. Like so many teams we were not sure what to expect; the event had only been agreed about eighteen months prior to the opening ceremony, which perhaps worked in our favour. Ever since then we have had time to plan, which should have been a good thing, apart for the fact that so have all the other teams in the world. Statistics can sometimes give a false impression, but unfortunately not in this case. The facts demonstrate that since 1987 the top rugby nations have all done so much better than Wales.

In 1991 we didn't even get through the group stages of the competition when we suffered an unexpected defeat at the hands of Western Samoa (now Samoa). Similarly in 1995 we were in the same group as New Zealand and lost by one point to Ireland, which put the seal on an early flight home from South Africa. Most recently we suffered in 2007 when Fiji defeated us by the odd couple of points in a seventy-plus-point match. In the other two World Cups the quarter-finals have been the limit of Welsh achievement.

So back to the glory days of 1987, where we arrived in Wellington, New Zealand, and had a few days to prepare for our opening group game against Ireland. We had one training session a day which lasted a couple of hours, plus a team meeting every two or three days to review things we'd done and plan for matches to come. Even though it doesn't sound much (it wasn't) there were still numerous players who moaned like hell (privately) about the amount of time they spent on the training pitches or in meeting rooms. Trips abroad, tours, had historically been regarded as a reward for a successful season or a reason to get together after a disappointing one, and we took our 'tour mentality' to the World Cup in 1987. We were not going to let a few games of rugby get in the way of a good time, and as we found ourselves sharing a hotel with the Irish team during the first week or so of the tournament we had our English-speaking Celtic brothers to play with. There were long hours to fill and we spent many of them fostering relations with the locals in pubs around the Wellington area. It seemed to work for us as we finished top of our group and then beat England, the old enemy from across the bridge, 16–3 in the quarter-final.

Both semi-finals were played in Australia, where we were well and truly beaten in Brisbane by New Zealand, undoubtedly the best team in the world at that time. This meant a third-place playoff match against Australia, who had been defeated by France in Sydney following a wonderful try by French full-back Serge Blanco in the dying minutes of the game.

Prior to the match we listened to an incredibly passionate

team talk delivered by our team manager Clive Rowlands. Clive is a wonderful character who deserves recognition for what he achieved in the game. His first game for Wales was against England and unusually he was appointed captain – indeed he captained Wales on each of the fourteen occasions he represented his country. After retiring from rugby he coached the Welsh team from 1968 to 1974, becoming the youngest person to hold the position. Those of you with good memories will recall this was a successful period in Welsh rugby history and included a Grand Slam in 1971. In fact he's the only person in the history of Welsh rugby to chalk up a grand slam of honours, becoming Welsh captain, coach, manager and Welsh Rugby Union president. He was and still is hugely respected and when he spoke we listened. You can't win a match based on desire and passion, but it certainly helps, and Clive had filled us with both during his team talk.

The only thing to surpass his speech was the level of support we received when we ran onto the pitch in Rotorua, not far from the Bay of Plenty in North Island New Zealand. I don't think rugby was played regularly at Rotorua and the pitch had been prepared especially for the playoff match. It reminded us of Pontypool Park in the valleys back in South Wales, as one side of the pitch was dominated by a huge bank, and on the bank were a handful of faithful Welsh supporters complete with red rugby shirts, flags and the occasional plastic daffodil. Far too few to generate the level of support we were greeted with. On the same bank were literally thousands of Maori people, the indigenous population of New Zealand, each and every one of them cheering for Wales. It gave me and the team a huge lift. The Australians must have felt extremely flat. They were devastated at having lost to France five days earlier and had practically no backing in the match against us.

The game itself was a very close affair and a touchline conversion from our full-back Paul Thorburn sealed a 22–21 victory in our favour. After the match we went over to the bank and applauded the supporters who had travelled from Wales to watch us play and also the tens of thousands of Maoris who had cheered and encouraged us from the first whistle to the last.

We arrived back in our changing rooms where we opened a couple of bottles of champagne to celebrate our third-place finish in the World Cup tournament. It was whilst sipping champagne I heard our young twenty-year-old back-row forward Richard Webster asking second row Robert Norster about the incredible Maori support we'd received. He obviously didn't want to appear foolish and quietly asked if there were historical links between Wales and the Maori population that he wasn't aware of.

'None that I can think of,' replied Bob.

'Well why were they all cheering us throughout the match?' asked Richard.

Bob started to laugh as he said, 'They don't like us Webby, they just hate the bloody Aussies.'

Road Warriors

John Hall

'John spent his entire rugby career with the famous Bath club. A formidable blind-side forward, he gained twenty-one England caps, a number which would have been greatly increased were it not for serious problems with the cartilage in his knees. Several operations during the latter half of his career resulted in lengthy spells on the side-lines.

'When the All Blacks toured the UK in 1983, the visitors rated him as the best forward they had encountered and when constructing his "Dream Team" video, England skipper Will Carling stated that John Hall would be the first player on his team sheet.

'I am absolutely sincere when I say it was

fortunate for me that John was coming to the end of his career as I was starting mine, although he would have undoubtedly taught me a lot in a relatively short space of time had we overlapped more. Whenever you mention John Hall's name to his peers in the rugby world you can tell from their response he was a man with immense talent and a "never say die" attitude towards the game.

To be honest the inaugural World Cup was little different from any other international tour in the eighties. It didn't seem to me we took the event very seriously and consequently the preparation was at best limited and certainly not very well thought through, especially by modern day standards. Having arrived at our destination, we were required to train for a couple of hours a day and attend the occasional team meeting. Apart from these minor inconveniences we were left to arrange our own entertainment to fill the bulk of the day.

The 1987 World Cup was hosted by Australia and New Zealand, with the England team starting their campaign at the Concord Oval in Sydney against Australia. We landed in Sydney and decamped into an exceptionally average hotel in Rushcutters Bay (the UK equivalent would be a Travel Lodge), sharing three to a room. In fairness we always shared rooms in those days (normally two to a room) but it highlights how things have changed when players today have individual rooms/suites. Within a few hours of landing we were required to board another flight to Brisbane for a training session and an official World Cup function. A great piece of organisation considering we had just completed the flight of thirty hours plus from the UK. When we arrived at the training ground most of the boys had to be woken up as we left the bus. Having participated in a piss-poor training session and shown our faces at the function, we were soon on the return flight to Sydney preparing to deal with the jetlag. In comparison, the 2003 England team landed in Australia almost four weeks before their opening game of the tournament; we arrived about four days prior to our first match.

During my playing days I was 6ft 3in tall, weighing in at about 17st. I was sharing with Steve Bainbridge, who was 6ft 7in and a similar weight to me, while the third member of the happy trio was Peter Winterbottom, the legendary open-side flanker who was very much the baby of the group in terms of size, at a mere 6ft 1in and a slight 15st. As you can appreciate there was not a lot of room to spare, particularly once all the kit and clothes necessary for the long campaign (hopefully) had been unpacked onto the floor. Three guys lying side by side on a standard double bed trying to watch TV is not perfect, particularly when one of them (Bainbridge) was moaning constantly about the lack of a children's TV channel. He had simple needs. To clarify, I should point out there was a pull-out bed under the sofa which was a great relief and meant we didn't all have to sleep in the double. It didn't take long for us to suss that it was important, vital even, for our sanity, to get out of the hotel and find some entertainment.

The plan was to go and see a bit of Sydney and Steve had the great idea of hiring some mopeds so we could get out and about and really experience the great city. He knew how to ride a bike, as did I, and we were confident Winters would get the knack of it pretty quickly. We utilised the Yellow Pages in the hotel room and found the address of a hire shop halfway to the Blue Mountains. After a couple of bus rides and a taxi we arrived at the bike shop, and met an Aussie genuinely called Bruce. We told him we were looking to hire some mopeds and potter around Sydney for a couple of days. He took one look at me and led me towards a full fairing FZ Yamaha 1200cc, one of the fastest road bikes in the world at that time. It is worth pointing out he had not at this stage asked any of us if we even had licences (we didn't). I was about to say that perhaps something a little smaller would be more appropriate, when Steve said, 'That looks fine for you Hally, what do you have for me, mate?' Bruce looked at Steve and decided as he was extremely tall he would be better off on an 850cc Honda or something equally ridiculous. Steve seemed pleased with his chariot and paid little attention to the Yamaha 125cc Bruce was sorting out for Winters, which in comparison to our mighty hogs looked like a child's first pushbike minus the stabilisers. After a minimal amount of paperwork we were on our way, at least Steve and I were – Winters seemed to be experiencing some difficulty in keeping up.

Whenever we arrived at a junction, Steve and I waited for our poor relation, who we later found out had never ridden a motorbike before. It was noticeable how little clutch control he had, which meant his apparent preferred method of leaving a junction was to pull a massive wheelie with a look of genuine fear on his face. We spent most of the day cruising around

Sydney visiting the sites and occasionally making unscheduled stops when our Yamaha 125cc specialist was pulled over by the police. Later in the day we decided to return to the hotel and show the boys our 'wheels'. Steve and I decided to race and see if we could get some of the touring party to witness the return of Peter 'Evel Knievel' Winterbottom. We were not far from our destination when a car pulled out of a junction, both of us slammed on the brakes, our respective back wheels locked up as we skidded to a halt inches away from the side panels of the car. My heart was racing as I got off my bike and walked towards the driver's side of the car. As this was the first occasion all day when an accident or near-accident had not been my fault I was going to deliver a massive bollocking to the miscreant.

I was about to grab hold of the door handle and yank it open when I saw the driver's face; he was not smiling, he was roaring with laughter. It was none other than the England No. 8 Dean Richards, who had decided on a more conventional means of transport to get around Sydney. It was at this point Winters arrived at the scene. He didn't (couldn't?) stop but just took one hand off the handlebars and waved two fingers in the direction of the three of us whilst looking straight ahead.

Minutes later we were at the hotel parking our bikes close to the entrance hoping the lads would see us dismount. Sadly the only person to witness our arrival was the England coach Martin Green, who informed us in no uncertain terms the bikes had to go back.

In the modern era practically every minute of every day is planned during a World Cup campaign, but in the late eighties during the first tournament we were often left to our own devices. With the wisdom of hindsight it is fair to say we made some very poor decisions.

As for me, I injured my knee a few days later and was sent home safe in the knowledge I was not about to be awarded an MBE for my services to rugby, or indeed motorbike riding.

Green Dragons

Jonathan Davies

'In the famous Max Boyce song "The Outside Half Factory" about a seam two miles underground where the outside halves are made, he describes a terrible tragedy in which one of the fitter's mates inadvertently breaks the mould, made of gold no less, that produced the legendary Barry John.

'Well, quite clearly they managed to repair the mould when they created a certain Jonathan Davies ("Jiffy"). He could control a game irrespective of whether his forwards had dominance or not. With most of his career played in the amateur era he soon caught the eye of rugby league clubs and controversially decided to sign for Widnes in 1988. He represented Wales and Great Britain in the league code of the sport before returning to union in 1995

when he signed for Cardiff. Eight years after his last rugby union cap he was selected to play for Wales against Australia, finishing his career in 1997 with a match against England.

'All rugby followers will see Jonathan on a regular basis either as a match commentator or analyst with the BBC. With his extensive knowledge of both codes he is a valuable member of the broadcast team, often predicting moves or patterns of play before they occur. Having spent many a "quiet night" with Jiffy over the years I can reliably inform readers he not only has an encyclopaedic knowledge of the sport, he also has a fantastic sense of humour – a true living legend.'

Never having been one to keep quiet when there was an opportunity to do otherwise, before I launch into my World Cup memory as per Lawrence's request, there is something I'd like to get off my chest. It concerns the relatively recent phenomenon of players who like to celebrate just prior to scoring a try and then, having grounded the ball, wait for their team-mates to congratulate them, slap them on the back, occasionally hug and sometimes even kiss them. This is one aspect of the modern game I'm pleased arrived after my own departure. In my day you put the ball down over the try line and depending on how far you'd run, you either jogged or walked back to your position praying you didn't throw up, knowing this was the only time you could guarantee the cameras would be focused on you. On the odd occasion a team-mate may have summoned up the energy to say, 'Well done' or 'Lucky bastard' on your return trip, he certainly wasn't going to run any unnecessary distance to congratulate you physically.

England's Chris Ashton made a few headlines in the most recent Six Nations Championship with what has become known as the 'Ash Splash'. One arm pointing straight ahead, the ball tucked under the other and a swallow dive Olympic hopeful Tom Daley wouldn't sniff at. However, to prove that there really is nothing new under the sun, I draw your attention to a Zimbabwean centre, Richard Tsimba, who took part in the 1987 World Cup. His trademark try was to launch himself at full speed skyward with his arms outstretched holding the ball in both hands, arc towards the try line and touch the ball down before landing on his head and completing a forward roll, all without any noticeable loss of pace. Sadly as he touched down for his second try against Romania in their group match in 1987, he discovered his angle of trajectory was marginally off, landing on his shoulder which instantly dislocated, ending his participation in the match. He did however apply downward pressure on the ball prior to the injury and the try stood. As he sat on the bench wrapped in a blanket, suffering immense pain, breathing gas and air, he must have been delighted to see his side lose 20–21. If anyone wants my advice, if you get over the try line, just put the ball down. There are no extra points for 'style'. There, lecture over. Now on to my story.

Although 1987 was a few years before professionalism, the Welsh Rugby Union made all the squad sign a document to the effect that we would not participate in any commercial activity, including the writing of articles or books for a period of six months after the conclusion of the tournament. The first match was New Zealand against Italy and the Welsh team settled down in the team room to watch the one-sided affair on television. There were more than a few comments from the boys when during the commercial break we saw Andy Dalton (the New Zealand World Cup captain who had been forced to pull out of the team days before the start due to injury, leaving David Kirk to lift the trophy a few weeks later) advertising 4 × 4 trucks. We reached the only possible conclusion we could; he was at the end of his career, injured, and had probably decided to cash in while his name still carried some weight. In the next commercial break we saw the All Blacks winger John Kirwan, who seconds earlier had been carving up the opposition with some breathtaking displays of speed and agility, advertising 'acne cream'. Dare I say he was 'spot on' in his delivery? Anyway, at twenty-two years of age he had his entire career ahead of him and unless he was promoting the cream for free (the Welsh boys did not subscribe to that theory) he was making money from his image eight years before the game became professional. It was obviously one set of rules for New Zealand and another for the Welsh.

Our last group game was against Canada at Invercargill in front of 14,000 spectators and I remember being made captain for the match, a proud moment for me. Leading up to the game I had a random thought about the respective team colours, as both Canada and ourselves played in red. Normally the visitors change their kit if there's a clash, but as we were both effectively playing away from home I wondered what would happen. The decision was made, both teams would bring two sets of shirts and the captains would toss a coin to decide. You can imagine how thrilled the boys were when I walked into the changing room and informed them we were playing in green. The fact we were making Welsh history in so doing seemed to have little impact on the disgruntled mob, so as captain I decided to try and put a different spin on the situation. I told them how the shirts were clearly going to become collectors' items and would probably be worth a fortune, if not immediately then in years to come. With no 4 × 4 trucks or acne cream to promote it was as close to making a few quid on the side as we were going to get. We thrashed Canada by eight tries to nil, and it was a great sight when the whistle blew for full time, to see the Canadians offering to swap shirts with none of the Welsh team prepared to accept.

At the official dinner later that night I had to say a few words as captain. I knew the Welsh management were slightly worried about what I might say, as they considered me a bit of a loose cannon. I think I put them at ease when I began by talking about the historical links between the two countries. Canada had ruled itself but had close commercial ties to the British Empire and was indeed a prominent member of the Commonwealth. Many Welsh rugby coaches had spent time in Canada over the years developing the sport and furthering international relations. I then moved onto the match; apart from 'hard luck' there's not a lot you can say about a forty-point drubbing, so I talked about the shirts.

'I know many of you were disappointed at not being able to swap shirts today,' I said, 'and that some of you were told the Welsh boys were not allowed to exchange shirts, while others were informed we only had two sets of kit for the tournament and as it looked as though we were now going to be staying in it longer than anticipated we had to hold on to them.

'The truth is we're all keeping our green shirts because we believe we'll get a much better price for them back home in Wales.'

The jaws of the Welsh management hit the floor. They couldn't believe someone would openly flout the laws of amateur rugby, particularly at an official function with them in the room. I smiled and said I was only joking and wouldn't dream of making money from the sport I loved so dearly. This may have placated the management but the entire squad knew what they were going to do with their shirts. Let's just say no Welshman who played that day is currently the owner of a unique green Welsh shirt. Only joking.

Stream of Consciousness

Gary Rees

‘Gary played his entire career at Nottingham, not a fashionable club, but having been born nearby in Long Eaton it seemed the natural destination for him and no one managed to persuade him to leave. Following retirement he has remained involved at Nottingham in a coaching capacity. One of the outstanding open-side flankers of his generation he played twenty-three times for England over a seven-year period, including two World Cups. It's testament to his durability when you consider he was up against the likes of Peter Winterbottom, Andy Robinson and later Neil Back, and still maintained a place in the England squad. Gary was always a relatively quiet man in the bar after a

match, but commanded huge respect from all those who came up against him on the pitch.

'While his story, as he admits himself, doesn't actually feature a World Cup incident, I felt it was just too good to miss out on.'

When Lawrence made contact with me regarding my World Cup memories I was delighted to help out but had one minor problem. Each story I supplied or suggested had already been submitted by another player from the same era. Having played in the first two World Cup competitions it appears I am severely lacking any original thought or material. I was keen to help but was informed that motorbikes and scuba-diving incidents from 1987 had already been covered, as had the kit debacle prior to the first match against New Zealand in 1991. So I decided to share my favourite story from my time as a player. It involves my debut game for the world-famous Barbarians. The tenuous link this story has to the World Cup is that many of the players who played in the game went on to represent their countries in World Cup campaigns. Not great, I know, but it is the best I could come up with.

With the sport of rugby becoming professional in 1995, the approach of the Barbarians had to move with the times, but I was lucky enough to play when the team literally 'turned up and turned out'. We never trained together, occasionally had a chat about what to do in certain areas of the pitch if awarded a penalty and very occasionally discussed what method of defence we would utilise. Many readers will remember the Baa Baas were known for one thing: open, running 'champagne' rugby. If we were in possession of the ball, no matter where it was on the field it was passed through the hands and we ran, even from behind our own try line. Whilst this provided great entertainment for the crowd it was absolutely knackering for the players on both sides. Having said that, it was a massive honour to be selected, and gave players the opportunity to play in the same team as other international players from all over the world. I always enjoyed observing the different styles of play and in particular meeting all the various characters.

My debut was made in the mid-eighties during the famous Easter Tour which sadly no longer takes place. The fixtures were against Penarth, Cardiff, Swansea and Newport and took place over the four-day Easter break, with Cardiff on the Saturday my introduction to the team. The Barbarians side on that occasion was captained by a French international, someone I had not previously met. It became clear during the briefest of team talks his command of English was comparable to my command of French (extremely limited). However, he didn't need to say much since we all knew the game plan. If we had the ball we ran, if they had it we were to do everything we could to get it back. Not rocket science, but effective.

Well, it should have been effective, but unfortunately due to a lack of familiarity between the players on the Barbarians team we managed to drop the ball consistently during the first half and found ourselves a few scores down by the break. I absolutely hated to lose any game, especially when a crowd of 25,000 were watching from the stands and many more at home on television. Back then we used to stay on the pitch during the interval, normally a couple of minutes, with a segment of orange followed by a few well-chosen words from the captain. As I walked towards the centre line I vividly remember thinking to myself, what on earth is he going to say to inspire a better second-half performance? He might well have been effective if we all spoke French, something I'll never know.

He beckoned us in by waving his arms and as we approached he pointed the index finger on his right hand skyward and moved it in a rapid circular motion at the same time saying something resembling, 'circle, circle, circle'. Fourteen of us formed a circle around the Frenchman as he indicated he wanted us to link arms and repeated the word 'tighter' several times. It was by no means conventional but I genuinely felt it was having the desired effect. I can only speak for myself, but the physical closeness of the boys as we ringed our leader made me feel very much part of the team and my desire to help my team-mates was increasing by the second. We all stared at the figure in the middle wondering if he was going to add a couple of words of advice to the physical motivation he had engendered.

At that moment, standing enclosed by the tight circle, he lifted the right leg of his shorts, and had a piss on the pitch with his team acting as a shield from the eyes of the paying public and TV cameras. He finished his business, put the 'little general' away and with a 'Gallic shrug', wave of his arm and a 'Merci', he made his exit from the circle ready for the second half. Leaving the rest of us looking at the pool of bubbles as the liquid soaked into the pitch.

Did we win the match? No, but it did provide me with a memory to last a lifetime.

Unaccustomed as I Am . . .

Finlay Calder

'Finlay represented Scotland from 1986 to 1991 gaining thirty-four caps, the last of which was against New Zealand in the 1991 World Cup. He is one of an extremely small number of men who have captained a successful British and Irish Lions tour, winning the 1989 series in Australia 2–1 despite losing the first Test. Some of the younger players on that tour went on to become seasoned campaigners on my first Lions trip in 1997; whenever references were made to previous Lions tours the name of Finlay Calder was always held in high regard as both a player and a leader.

'Those of you who remember seeing Finlay play will recall he was not the fastest of back-row forwards,

but his understanding of the game was second to none and more often than not he was in the right place at the right time in both attack and defence. Finlay was a hugely respected player who was not averse to giving his opposite number, or indeed any member of the opposition, a "gentle" reminder that he was around. If I were to describe him in one word it would be "uncompromising".

'Interestingly, Finlay's twin brother Jim also played for Scotland (twenty-seven caps) and toured with the Lions in 1983. However, their international careers never overlapped as Jim retired the year before Finlay was selected (in truth he was dropped aged twenty-seven, but retirement sounded more dignified).'

I have very fond memories of the inaugural World Cup. It was played whilst the game was still well and truly amateur and the Scottish approach along with every other team in the tournament, with the exception of New Zealand, reflected this.

There was nothing the Scottish Union could do about the location of the 1987 World Cup; New Zealand will always remain on the other side of the world, some 12,000 miles from Scotland. They could, however, have put some thought into the journey and perhaps how we were to prepare for the tournament on arrival. In true Scottish style our finest team of rugby players departed for the first-ever World Cup and spent close to fifty hours travelling economy class to New Zealand. The reason it took so long was due to delays somewhere in Asia and also the fact we couldn't land in Christchurch on account of the weather. Unfortunately no one had made the pilot aware of this fact until we arrived just above Christchurch. He circled the airport a few times and then turned the plane back to Auckland to make his landing. The team were safe but about 600 miles away from where we needed to be. After several more hours hanging around we took another flight and completed our journey.

We arrived at the team hotel midway through the afternoon and were informed we had thirty minutes to check in, get our training kit on and meet in reception. Once the bleary-eyed troops reconvened we climbed aboard a bus and were taken to our first training session. To be fair it was described as a 'bit of a loosener', no more than a run around to help get the journey out of our systems, just some stretching and touch rugby. Personally, I think a few hours in bed getting some rest would have been the better option. I've reflected on this World Cup with several players from Scotland and other countries and the consensus seems to be, everything was done with the best of intentions but looking back there were some crazy decisions made by management teams and coaches. Put simply, everything was not just amateur, it was amateurish.

Professionalism, of course, still being some way into the future, we received no pay for our endeavours but all the players were given NZ$12 per day to cover incidental expenses and phone calls home. Not a huge amount but when saved up over the course of a week it did mean cocktail night every Wednesday was quite a lively affair for the majority of the squad and the occasional invited guest.

Our last match in the group stage was against Romania in Dunedin and this game saw Colin Deans, our hooker, win his fiftieth cap, a very rare achievement back in the eighties. We arrived at the ground and had our customary pitch inspection. Looking back, I have no idea why we used to do this. It certainly didn't prepare us for the atmosphere, as the stadium would have been less than 10 per cent full at the time. Some people think it provided us with the opportunity to look at the state of the playing surface so we could adjust our footwear or length of studs accordingly. In reality most of us had one pair of boots for matches, and an older pair for training (no spare studs). Fancy Dans might have had a pair with moulded studs in case the ground was really hard, but that was about it. The truth of the 'pitch inspection' is we always arrived early for matches because the management 'snag time' was never required and it gave us something to do before kick-off.

We had a hard-fought battle against Romania, particularly in the first half, but by the final whistle we had run away with it 55–28. As we'd drawn with France in our first match we needed a healthy points tally to try and qualify in first place and thereby avoid New Zealand in the quarter-finals. Without the benefit of mobile phones we didn't find out the score from the French match for some time, but at least we were through (France hammered Zimbabwe and took top spot in the group). We were all gathered in our changing room deep in the bowels of the main stand at Carisbrook, when Roy Laidlaw, our scrum-half, asked all the lads to take a seat. He was going to make a presentation to Colin in recognition of reaching the significant milestone in caps.

Roy was not particularly comfortable speaking in public but I have to say he did an amazing job. He delivered one of the most meaningful, touching and heartfelt speeches I have ever heard. He expressed what an absolute credit Colin had been to his country and what a pleasure, indeed honour, it had been for many of us to play alongside him for so many years. There was hardly a dry eye in the changing room when Roy asked Colin to come up and receive a gift which the entire squad had contributed to (we must have cut down on the cocktail budget that particular week). No one moved. Initially I thought the emotion of the occasion had got to Colin and he was probably trying to compose himself before going up to receive his gift. A couple of seconds later Gavin Hastings and one or two others burst out laughing, which to be honest I didn't feel was appropriate behaviour. I glared at Gavin, who actually had tears rolling down his cheeks as he said to Roy Laidlaw, 'Did you not think to check whether Colin was here before making your speech?' We all looked around and the only member of the squad missing from the changing room was Colin Deans.

When Colin arrived a few minutes later, Roy delivered a similar speech but the moment had gone, the boys had moved on from sincerity to taking the piss. As I write these words I can still see the changing room, the spot where Roy was standing as he spoke, and I smile as I remember just how wonderfully amateur it all was in those days.

Let Loose

Nigel Redman

'Nigel managed to play 349 games for Bath Rugby over a sixteen-year period. He gained twenty England caps and was dropped on no fewer than eleven occasions. Unfortunately for Nigel he was "only" a fraction over 6ft 3in, which for a second row is not considered tall enough. Whenever he toured with England he would often arrive back in the UK as England's No. 1 due to his immense athleticism and ball-handling skills. Sadly, several weeks after returning from tour, when his name came up in selection he would be deemed too small and therefore spent more time playing for his beloved Bath than he should have.

'Apart from the numerous cup and league victories he achieved with his club, one of his personal

highlights was being called into the 1997 Lions tour to South Africa whilst on yet another England tour to Argentina. His coach in Argentina was Jack Rowell, and when he broke the news to Nigel of his selection, Nigel looked at him with complete shock on his face and said, 'I don't believe it,' to which Jack replied, 'No, neither do I.' He assumes Jack's disbelief was down to his sadness at the loss of Nigel for the remainder of the Argentinian tour and not the simple fact he just couldn't get his head round the idea that the Lions had requested Nigel. I think it's probably best not to investigate that any further. Having arrived in South Africa Nigel captained a midweek Lions team to victory (52–30) against Orange Free State – an unbeaten Lions captain? There are surely not many of those knocking around the rugby world.

'Nigel is still very much involved in rugby as Elite Coaching Manager at the Rugby Football Union.'

When Lawrence asked if I had a particular World Cup memory suitable for inclusion in this book, it occurred to me there was not one specific incident or occasion that stood out. What I have is a host of memories leading up to and throughout the event which highlight the difference between the amateur era and the modern professional approach. It may not be what you asked for, Lol, but it's what you're going to get.

The year of the first World Cup was a memorable one for me. I proposed to the current Mrs Redman, we bought our first house together, and I equalled the record of tries scored in a Cup final during Bath's win over Wasps at Twickenham – not bad for a second row, although the record, if I'm honest, doesn't stand much scrutiny in terms of inducing jaw-dropping awe: it was two tries, there are about fifteen other players with whom I share the distinction, and I am not even the only second row on the list, as my team-mate Martin Haag also scored a double in the 1995 final, again against Wasps; mind you, a record is a record as far as I am concerned. Added to that, as a member of an England squad successful in only one match of the Five Nations Championship I gained selection to participate in the first-ever World Cup tournament. The next challenge was how to take six weeks off work without losing my job as an electrician. I decided honesty was the best policy and fessed up to my employers that in my spare time I was in fact an England international rugby player. This came as something of a surprise to them. Apparently they had never noticed my previous sojourns, thanks entirely to my work colleagues who brilliantly covered for me during domestic international matches when I was away for a couple of days. I like to think that was the reason the powers-that-be were unaware of my disappearances, rather than the quality of my work being eminently missable. Having explained about the World Cup, the existence of which had passed most people by back then, they kindly agreed to a leave of absence. Unpaid, of course.

The international season had got off to a stuttering start with the opening fixture against Scotland at Twickenham postponed due to a frozen pitch, meaning our first match of the campaign would be against Ireland at Lansdowne Road. In fairness we didn't do too much in the way of pre-match analysis in those days. It was generally left to the people who had experience of playing against the up-coming opponents to give an appraisal of what to expect. 'It'll be wet and windy, the Irish will kick everything just above grass level, occasionally below it, and the crowd will be on our backs from the start.' I can't remember who actually said those words but it might as well have been Mystic Meg as it was absolutely correct. The rain never ceased, I had the shit kicked out of me, the crowd were against us for eighty minutes (although later that evening as I entered the Dublin nightlife they were like long-lost friends) and we lost the match 17–0. Possibly the first time England ever failed to score in a Test. I became a casualty of the post-match analysis (we had those unfortunately) and was dropped for the next two games, France at Twickenham and Wales in Cardiff, the latter becoming notorious for the violence which took place. Mike Teague, the Gloucester and England No. 8, was targeted from the kick-off, fight followed fight, and Wade Dooley, the English lock, hurt his hand when Phil Davies put his jaw in the way of Wade's swinging arm (apparently this incident also led to Phil unluckily sustaining a broken jaw). Wales won the match and England suspended Richard Hill (captain), Gareth Chilcott, Graham Dawe and the aforementioned Wade Dooley. Some felt the decision was harsh, but with Dooley on the sidelines the door opened for my return in the rearranged fixture against Scotland at Twickenham, a match England dominated from the first whistle to the last and in which I performed well enough to gain selection for the World Cup.

In preparation for the tournament the Rugby Football Union made a revolutionary decision and hired the services of an athletics coach called Tom McNab. (Interestingly when looking at Tom's extensive website recently, I noticed that this appointment warrants less than one line and is buried away under several subheadings.) Tom is a Scot, a best-selling author and was technical director on the Oscar-winning film *Chariots of Fire*, but even for someone with such an impressive pedigree it was an almost impossible task to increase the athleticism of the England World Cup squad. As we prepared on the running tracks of England Tom could be heard shouting his favourite catchphrases, 'Relax and run with a jelly jaw,' or 'Run as if you are holding a delicate crisp between your fingers.' All the talk of jelly and crisps was too much for some who followed a strenuous session with a visit to the bar to celebrate getting under 30 per cent body fat. Another of Tom's favourite quotes was, 'you can't fire a cannon from a canoe,' in reference to building a solid training base. Highly reflective by nature, I remember responding to this by pointing out to Tom you could fire a cannon from a canoe if it was fired along its length. I like to think I am slightly less anally-retentive these days.

By early May we were as ready as we were ever going to be and departed from our hotel to Heathrow. The adventure had begun. I'd never previously flown long haul, never been on a jumbo jet, and was excited at the prospect of stopping off in Bahrain and Singapore en route. 'Do you think we'll get our passports stamped?' I remember asking one of the more experienced tourists. On entering the plane the stewardess (yes, those were the days when they were called stewardesses, trolley dollies, coffee jockeys, wagon dragons and the rest) was guiding first-class passengers to the left whilst ensuring our squad were heading towards 'economy'. I had been told prior to departure that the

RFU had a policy on seats with leg room and that at 6ft 3in and 17st I was neither tall enough nor big enough to qualify. The pre-booked emergency exit seats with additional legroom were for the 'big lads' only. Surely I had a chance of an aisle seat? No such luck. A window? No, I was wedged in between fly-half Rob Andrew and winger Rory Underwood, both about 5ft 8in and neither prepared to swap seats. By the time we'd all had the compulsory giggle at the stewardess demonstrating how to 'top up' the air in our life jackets by blowing into the hose, I knew it was going to be a hot, increasingly smelly and uncomfortable flight to the other side of the world. The journey was broken up into eight-hour flying slots with about an hour stop-over in Bahrain and Singapore and no they wouldn't be stamping my passport. We eventually landed at Sydney airport before flying up to Brisbane for a training session and the opening ceremony. Approximately thirty hours after leaving Heathrow we arrived at our hotel.

'Drop your bags in your rooms and be on the bus in half an hour, changed and ready to train,' came the instructions from England coach Martin Green. We arrived at our training ground, the GPS club, where the first task of the duty boys was to move up and down the bus in an effort to wake all the sleeping players. The conditions were hot and humid, which combined with the damp air made breathing difficult. My most notable memory from the first session was a tackling practice where the tackling players were asked to kneel on the grass and as luck would have it they positioned themselves over a colony of large and overly aggressive ants. Training continued after the medics had used up their supply of camomile and antihistamine.

Following the opening ceremony we were back on the bus and

heading for the airport to fly south to our Sydney base, a motel (yes, MOTEL) in Rushcutters Bay. This is an area on the outskirts of the red-light district known as Kings Cross, and our motel was situated about 400 metres from its centre. The accommodation had seen better days, the restaurant was on the top floor, and a tenpin bowling alley and burger bar featured in reception. At the back of the motel there was a small kidney-shaped pool and our training pitch.

The keys were handed out and my room-mate and great friend Graham Dawe and I made our way to room 101. As depicted in George Orwell's *1984*, were we to be made to confront our worst fears? Oh yes. On opening the door any mild excitement we may have had soon evaporated. The room was on the small side, damp, with a settee and one double bed. 'Do you want to toss a coin for the bed or wrestle for it?' I asked Dawsey. After crashing around for five minutes we decided to take it in turns. The room also had a large window overlooking our training pitch and a small bathroom with a warmish shower that distributed water powerfully at a rather inconvenient 90° angle to the floor.

Towards the end of our first full day in Sydney, as I left the tenpin bowling alley I was greeted by the loud roar of motorbike engines ridden by fellow lock forward Steve Bainbridge and back-row forwards John Hall and Peter Winterbottom. John goes into more detail about this story elsewhere in this book so I will mention it only in passing. Apparently Winterbottom had never been on a bike before and had to borrow Dave Egerton's driving licence in order to hire the 125cc chopper he was proudly sitting astride. It was probably no more than ten seconds between the three of them turning off their engines and Martin Green telling them to return the bikes to the hire shop. 'But Martin, we've got them for three days.' Martin just glared and without another word they started their 'hogs' and took them back.

We were scheduled to play Australia, followed by Japan and the USA in the group stage. The selectors decided to keep faith with the team that had beaten Scotland, a personal landmark for me as it was the first time I'd been selected for two consecutive England internationals (having made my debut three years earlier). We played our three group matches at the Concord Oval, the home of West Harbour RFC. We were competitive in our opener against Australia going down 19–6, the turning point a hotly disputed try by David Campese. The fact he bounced the ball off his knee as he crossed the try line made no impact on New Zealand referee Keith Lawrence. Feeling hard done by, the squad boarded a plane bound for Hamilton Island, a leading resort destination in the Whitsunday Islands for a couple of days' R & R. The highlight of our stay was a visit to the beautiful Great Barrier Reef. The players and management were given the choice of either flying out to the reef in a helicopter and snorkelling, or going by boat to a small island reef and scuba diving. I had always wanted to scuba dive and opted for the boat trip along with my Bath team-mates Graham Dawe, Richard Hill and Gareth Chilcott. When the two groups met later that evening to exchange stories it became apparent only two of the touring party had come close to dying.

From the helicopter group, Martin Green, the head coach, stood up on a boat, stripped off his shirt, fitted his mask and snorkel and said, 'I have been waiting all my life for this moment,' before diving into the sea, not realising the water was only twelve inches deep and the rest of the party already in the water were lying on top of the reef. Martin badly grazed his chest and legs on the live coral and, after being coated with bright orange iodine spray (he probably needed some camomile, but the doc's supply had already been used), was left feeling very uncomfortable for a number of days. Meanwhile on our trip, while removing his air tank and buoyancy control device, Graham Dawe had forgotten he was wearing a 15kg lead-weighted belt, which resulted in him disappearing into a cloud of bubbles heading rapidly to the bottom of the reef, to reappear like a frightened cat some time later with his weight belt remaining on the sea bed.

After our adventures on the Reef we returned to Sydney, beat Japan, where I scored my one and only international try, rolled over the USA and booked our place in the quarter-finals, where we were to meet our good friends from Wales.

After being rested for the USA match the selectors were obviously so impressed by my try-scoring efforts against the mighty Japanese that I found myself selected for the Welsh game. My second-row partner was 6ft 8in PC Dooley, who had now completed his suspension following the match in Cardiff. Martin Green informed me I would be jumping in the middle of the line-out against Welsh legend Bob Norster, adding that it should be a fair contest as Bob had a hamstring injury. In addition to Bob's ailments Wales had also lost a prop and a back-row forward to injury and had invited the teenage pair Dai Young and Richard Webster to join the squad. Dai and Richard were on holiday backpacking around Australia when they saw a request for them to contact the Welsh management in a newspaper article.

At the first team meeting we established our strategy for the match. Dominate the Welsh physically up front, starting with the first scrum where we were to target the backpacker Young. 'First scrum on our ball, let's hold the ball at the No. 8's feet and double shunt them with all eight forwards driving on,' was the advice of Gareth Chilcott, who was starting the match on the bench, followed by, 'Let's teach this young f***** what international rugby is all about.' Training went pretty well during the week and at the end of our final team meeting England manager Mike Weston announced that the winner of the match would be staying in Brisbane to play their semi-final, while the loser would be on the 6.30 a.m. flight back to London the following day. We had to pack our bags and leave them in our rooms before departing for the game, not knowing whether we would be flying back to the UK or not.

According to the military, 'No plan survives first contact with the enemy.' This statement could just as well be applied to the sport of rugby union, as within five minutes of the kick our mighty pack was being driven backwards at an unbelievable rate of knots, as our No. 8 Dean Richards attempted a complicated back-row move. Just before half-time, our loose-head prop Paul Rendall collapsed with an eye injury leaving me to volunteer for front-row duties five metres from our own line. Our seven forwards manfully packed down against the full quota of eight Welshmen, we put the ball in and just before my head disappeared up my backside I saw the ball roll out of the scrum where we should have had a flanker and noticed Welsh open-side Gareth Roberts diving onto the ball to score for Wales. And that was our best moment: Wales scored two more tries through John Devereux and Robert Jones and we lost our quarter-final 16–3.

Our World Cup was over and I was left rueing the fact I was (only) 6ft 3in and would soon be wedged into an economy seat for the flight home.

For those of you wondering about my career development, now the cat was out of the bag with regard to my rugby moonlighting, to their credit my employers took it in their stride, after a touch of gentle persuasion. I mentioned earlier I was anally retentive, so much so that the next year, prior to a six-week England tour which was to be followed by a month-long trip with Bath, I prepared a presentation highlighting the positive aspects of having an employee who represented his country at rugby union. I made a solid business case, laced with corporate benefits and my personal development, concluding with the additional profile my position in the sporting world would bring to the company.

Once again they agreed to let me take the time off, which I have to say was very decent of them, but I am not sure they would have been quite so accommodating had they realised I was to be forced to spend the week in between the two trips recuperating from my England excesses, snoozing my way through the day while I should have been rewiring the Bristol Royal Infirmary A&E department. I was able to undertake this much-needed recovery process by sitting at the top of a long pair of step ladders, my upper half out of sight through a gap in the ceiling tiles, with my head resting on a joist and my eyes firmly shut. The disembodied legs dangling limply down which greeted the sick and injured on their arrival to the waiting room can hardly have instilled much confidence in the healing powers of the casualty medical staff. Happy days indeed.

Vague Memory

David Sole

'Many prop forwards enter their prime as they turn thirty years of age; David Sole retired from international rugby aged thirty. He had however accumulated forty-four caps for Scotland, twenty-five as captain, plus a British and Irish Lions tour by this time.

'Richard Bath said in his book *The Complete Book of Rugby*, "David Sole is another of those players who is remembered and virtually defined by one moment: in this case it was when he made the decision for his side to take the now famous walk onto the pitch for the Grand Slam decider against England at Murrayfield in 1990. As a statement of resolve, it was a masterstroke from which the English never recovered as they lost the most high-

profile game in Five Nations Rugby history. It also cemented Sole's name in Scottish folklore ..."

'He will also be remembered for another match against England when he played with his left shirt sleeve removed so the English tight-head prop Jeff Probyn could not grab it to gain some perceived advantage. Conversely Jeff was happy to see David paying more attention to him than he was to his own game.

'These moments may define David Sole's career to some extent, but it does him a disservice to say they encapsulate his playing days entirely. Due to his "early" retirement from rugby our playing careers didn't overlap, but I do remember watching him play; he was an extremely mobile prop who was so quick he played in the Scotland sevens team, and believe me there are not many props who can claim the honour of representing their country in this version of the game.'

The Scottish team arrived in Christchurch for our first group match against France and after a couple of days getting over jetlag and a few training sessions we felt ready for the challenge. The day before the match a few of us were relaxing in the team room watching some rubbish on TV. At the bottom of the screen was a box with some 'rolling news'.

There were two lines of script and they read as follows – Auckland 15 Rotorua 14 . . . Wellington 13 Nelson Marlborough 12 . . . Christchurch 10 Dunedin 10 . . . Invercargill 11 Milford Sound 10 etc.

One of the squad who shall remain nameless (he has a brother called Scott Hastings) walked into the team room and stared at the screen for a few moments, taking in the names and numbers before saying to the boys, 'Wow those were all bloody close games.' Everyone in the team room stared at the individual, let's call him Gav for the purpose of this story, with looks of absolute disbelief on their faces. Realising he was serious, not one of us even bothered to tell Gav he was looking at the weather forecast and the numbers related to temperatures in the relevant New Zealand towns and cities.

On the field of play the real matches were brutal to put it mildly. To refresh your memory, the squad size in 1987 was twenty-five players and only two replacements were allowed during a match. Following a 20–20 draw against France in our opening game, the Scottish management decided it would help our campaign if we could go on and win the group, thereby missing an almost certain quarter-final against New Zealand. A consequence of this decision was to field a broadly similar team barring injury, for every match (our best team), which meant little rest for those selected. We picked up a few injuries against France and a couple more during a relatively comfortable 60–21 victory over Zimbabwe. In order to finish top we needed a decent win against Romania so the strongest team available was once again selected. Romania were a much better team in the late eighties than they are now, we knew they'd be difficult to break down and, having lost to them three years earlier, several players reminded the rest of the lads just how physical the match was likely to be.

Scott Hastings had pulled his hamstring in a warm-up game of touch rugby prior to the tournament starting and this was to be his first match of the World Cup. Someone may have a more accurate memory than mine but I recall he pulled his hamstring again about six seconds after the whistle was blown to start the match, ending his participation in the tournament. Thinking about it now, Scott may well hold the world record for the shortest time spent on a rugby pitch in international rugby. He definitely travelled further than anyone for a few seconds of participation in a World Cup. Shortly after Scott was replaced, our big lock forward Alan Tomes picked up a shoulder injury and also had to leave the field. Within minutes we'd used our two replacements and therefore couldn't afford any further injuries. Shortly after half-time the game was still very much in the balance, we were leading by six or seven points but needed to press on and try to get a decent score. This was the point when our open-side flanker John Jeffrey managed to get himself concussed (not an easy diagnosis to make in John's case).

We couldn't allow JJ to leave the pitch, the team would be down to fourteen men and more worryingly the pack would be down to seven against the huge Romanian forwards. We all gathered around as the trainer applied the 'magic sponge' to JJ's head and listened to Colin Deans, our captain, issue his instructions. When Romania had a scrum, he decided, JJ would go to No. 8 and Iain Paxton would move to open side. This meant if they tried any back-row moves someone who had a brain still working would become the first line of defence, scrum-half Roy Laidlaw would then arrive on the scene to further disrupt the move, leaving JJ a little more time to 'get in the way' shortly afterwards. I clearly remember Colin saying to JJ, 'Are you okay?' to which he replied, 'Aye, no problem.' He then asked if he was happy switching to No. 8. Again the reply, 'No problem.'

As we made our way towards the next scrum I felt a tap on my shoulder. Turning to my right I saw a slightly dazed John Jeffrey looking quizzically at me. 'Soley, what's No. 8?' I tried to find a plus side of this encounter. At least he could remember my name. But I knew we had a real problem when he followed this up with, 'Where are we?'

'We're in Dunedin, New Zealand. Are you sure you're okay?' He delivered the usual forward's response, 'Yeah, yeah, I'm fine. Just a little bit fuzzy, that's all.' As we reached the scrum he leant over and quietly whispered in my ear, 'What the f*** are we doing in New Zealand?'

For the record, the above is true and John remained on the pitch for the entire match, scoring three tries in our 55–28 victory. To this day he has no recollection of the entire occasion.

Unfortunately the Scottish team still came second in the group and then lost to New Zealand in the quarter-final, while France faced Fiji and went on to contest the final against New Zealand a couple of weeks later. If JJ had managed just a couple more tries, who knows? It could have been us! Perhaps in his confused state we should have told him he was John Kirwan to see what might have happened.

1991

The 1991 Rugby World Cup was hosted in the northern hemisphere. With England as main hosts, various matches throughout the tournament were also dispersed around Scotland, Wales, Ireland and France, the final being held at Twickenham. Each country wanted a slice of the action so nineteen venues in total were scheduled for fixtures. The second Rugby World Cup saw the emergence of non-IRFB members onto the world stage.

The tournament once again featured sixteen teams pitted against each other. This time, however, a qualification process involving thirty-three nations had been introduced from which emerged Argentina, Western Samoa, Japan, Italy, Romania, Canada, Zimbabwe and the USA to compete alongside the seven IRFB members. South Africa was once more excluded. Fiji filled the remaining space thanks to their advancement to the quarter-final stage of the 1987 competition.

Hosts England kicked off the opening match against

defending champions New Zealand on 3 October. The All Blacks won by a small margin, 18–12, but at least the England performance was of a far more advanced and confident nature than had been evident in their matches four years previously.

Perhaps still complacent from their third-place glory of 1987, Wales encountered outsiders Western Samoa at Cardiff Arms Park. The match is still regarded as one of the biggest upsets in the tournament's history, and in many ways encapsulated the spirit of the Rugby World Cup. With brutal tackling, strong attacking play and steely determination, the supposed minnows triumphed over one of the bigger fish with a 16–13 victory. One of the visions for the World Cup had been to open up the game to developing rugby nations, thereby nurturing a wider rugby community. Western Samoa grasped the opportunity on offer heroically, and emerged onto the world stage in a blaze of glory.

So it was Australia and Western Samoa who progressed from Wales's pool and they were joined in the quarter-finals by New Zealand, England, Scotland, Ireland, France and Canada. The latter team, also regarded as having minnow status, overcame Fiji and Romania to make it into the remaining eight and only narrowly lost to France. If further evidence was required that the ethos of the World Cup was working, here it was.

Impressive as the outsiders' efforts were, both teams would unfortunately crash back down to earth at the next hurdle. Canada, against defending champions New Zealand, fought bravely but were defeated 29–13, and Home Nation Scotland succeeded where Wales could not, defeating the Western Samoan debutants with a 28–6 victory. England continued their success, progressing into the semi-finals following a superb 19–10 win over the French in Paris. This quarter-final saw the ninety-third and final appearance by Serge Blanco, the French hero who had been superb four years earlier in France's semi-final victory against Australia.

The most impressive quarter-final saw favourites Australia take on Ireland at their home ground, Lansdowne Road, Dublin. In a tightly contested match the Aussies, just five minutes from time, trailed the Home Nation 18–15. Regarded as one of the best matches of the tournament, Ireland lost out in the final minute after the Australian fly-half Michael Lynagh literally bounced over the line to give Australia a 19–18 victory and a place in the semi-finals for the second time in a row.

England met their oldest foe Scotland in the first semi-final. Despite maintaining ball possession and dominating territory, full-back Jonathan Webb's unreliable kicking ensured the scoreboard did not reflect England's dominance (that's how I remember it anyway). Only a dropped goal from the disciplined boot of Rob Andrew secured the game for England 9–6. This is the furthest Scotland have progressed to date and they would end up finishing fourth after losing the third-place playoff.

As four years previously, the 1991 final featured a northern versus southern hemisphere battle. In front of a capacity crowd at Twickenham, England and Australia contested the match and for both it was unfamiliar territory.

In the final England adopted an open, running style but failed to crack the Australians. Yet they came close and had it not been for a controversial incident in the second half, the outcome might have been very different. Facing a 12–3 deficit, England had secured an attacking overlap and as Peter Winterbottom passed to winger Rory Underwood the ball was knocked down by David Campese. Many perceived this was a deliberate knock-on, designed to prevent an England score. The English camp argued for a penalty try, insisting that Underwood would have easily made it over the line. However the referee, Welshman Derek Bevan, awarded only a penalty. Jonathan Webb converted his second penalty of the game but no further England points were to follow.

Despite the controversy of the final, David Campese had made his mark on the wing and was arguably the star of the competition. Ultimately the better team on the day (true, I'm afraid), and the best throughout the competition, Australia were rewarded for their efforts as captain Nick Farr-Jones lifted the Webb Ellis Cup.

Though doubts may have remained about the future of the Rugby World Cup following the initial tournament in 1987, the 1991 competition guaranteed the event a place on the international sporting calendar. It was an unquestionable success, and captured the imagination of a television audience of 1.75 billion viewers compared with 300 million in

1987. If there had been even a glimmer of doubt before, it had now been firmly extinguished. The Rugby World Cup was here to stay.

A Dish Best Served Cold

The 1991 tournament was much more of an event for me than that of four years previously. Having started to play rugby at school and then joined Wasps in 1990, I knew the sport was going to play a significant part in my life. The England team had gone on a bit of a march following the appointment of Geoff Cooke as manager/coach, completing a Five Nations Grand Slam in the World Cup year. England were captained by Will Carling, whose partner in the centre was an even younger lad called Jeremy Guscott. Little did I know at the time as I watched the matches on television that Jerry and I were destined to become international team-mates and partners in crime during numerous off-field misdemeanours.

The stage was set. New Zealand were the world champions having won the tournament four years earlier on home soil, so surely it was now primary host England's turn to reign. At the time I had no idea which body of stuffed shirts was responsible for organising the tournament, but there couldn't have been an Englishman amongst them, as we were given that opening game at Twickenham against the holders. The

12–18 defeat was hardly the ideal start to the campaign but comfortable victories against Italy and the USA meant England finished second in the group, qualifying for the knockout stages.

Anyone who watched the quarter-final against France in Paris will remember perhaps the defining moment. English winger Nigel Heslop was on the wrong end of a mighty wallop delivered by the French back-row forward Eric Champ, who had taken offence to his (slightly) late tackle on the French hero and full-back Serge Blanco. Nigel has no recollection of what happened next or indeed anything else that took place during the rest of the day, but the image of England's newly appointed 'enforcer', Mick 'The Munch' Skinner, standing eyeball-to-eyeball with Champ and Champ taking a step backward, will remain with me for ever. In any environment, and rugby in particular, it's a great feeling when you know your team-mates are prepared to step up to the plate and look out for you (although sadly a little late for Nigel on that particular day).

I will always take a 19–10 victory away from home against France and it was with a degree of confidence the team headed to Scotland and Murrayfield for the semi-final against the Auld Enemy. Once again the match provided the viewers with a memorable moment. The match was finely balanced at 6–6 when Scotland were awarded a penalty twenty metres from the English try line, slightly to the right of the posts. The Scottish full-back Gavin Hastings stepped up to take a kick which would give the Scots a potential match-winning advantage in what was a very tight contest. Gavin scored 667 points for Scotland during his long and illustrious international career, a total which would have been 670 had he not missed that kick on 26 October 1991 (bless you, Gav). The door had been left open for England and Rob Andrew duly walked through it with a late drop to secure a 9–6 victory.

Everything was going to script, England had reached the World Cup final, with more good news the following day as New Zealand went down 16–6 to Australia at Lansdowne Road. Surely we could defeat Australia with our forward dominance? England had spent the entire tournament relying on their huge pack to grind down the opposition, which together with the reliable boot of Rob Andrew had proved a winning formula. Bizarrely they threw this game plan out of the window for the final, instead opting for a more open, expansive, running style in a bid to crack the Australians. A bad decision as it turned out, confirmed by the 12–6 final scoreline in favour of captain Nick Farr-Jones and his men.

Many years later, I spoke to the Australian rugby legend John Eales about the 1991 final. John is quite simply the most successful captain in his nation's history. It's well known in rugby circles he used to have the nickname 'Nobody' because nobody's perfect. He played eighty-six times for Australia, notching up an incredible 173 points in the process. Even more impressively, he has two World Cup winning medals, from 1991 and 1999, the second as captain. For the Twickenham final John was a mere pup in terms of his international career and as he recalled when we were chatting, the English support had a big impact on him that day.

'I can distinctly remember running onto the pitch for the final. Given my tender years and the enormity of the occasion I had never experienced a crowd atmosphere like it. The stadium was filled with the sound of "Swing Low Sweet Chariot" and apart from a small but vociferous pocket of gold Australian shirts, tucked away in the seats with a restricted view, it seemed as though only one set of supporters had been allowed to enter the ground. As we lined up to start the game I looked over at our captain Nick Farr-Jones, who nodded his head and gave me a big smile which had a calming effect on me. At the time my interpretation was him saying, "Enjoy yourself, I have every confidence in you." Years later, having had experience of the captaincy myself, I believe he was probably saying, "You're young and raw, for God's sake don't stuff it up."'

England may have shot themselves in the foot to some extent with their change of tactics for the final, but it is clear from John's recollections of the Australian changing room afterwards that the boys in white gave it everything they had.

'It actually represented something more akin to a war zone with players lying around on the benches and the floor, physically and mentally exhausted. When I was growing up I'd played in finals of rugby and cricket tournaments and experienced the joy of winning and the pain of defeat. But it was only after the 1991 World Cup ended that it struck what this of all finals meant. One game to determine how you and your team would be judged in years to come. All the work came down to eighty minutes after which you were either a world champion, or not. Whatever way it goes, your life will never be quite the same again.'

John is spot on here in his description of the emotions that come with victory or defeat in a World Cup final. I know, I've experienced both, although it took us 100 minutes to enjoy the sweet taste of success. But more of that later.

One individual who played in the 1991 final was also a member of the England team that won the World Cup twelve years later, Jason Leonard. In his words he remained in international rugby long enough to put right the wrong of 1991. He wanted his revenge and he was going to hang around as long as he possibly could to get it. Another player I want to mention from 1991 is Brian Moore, England's combative hooker. Known as 'The Pitbull', Brian is a seriously competitive individual who physically gave everything he had in that second World Cup final, and ended up with a loser's medal for his efforts. The medal remained at home for a year or two, but every time he opened the drawer in which he had stashed it he was reminded of the defeat, so one day he placed it in his pocket, went for a walk and threw it into the River Thames. Following the England victory in 2003 Brian freely admits to a feeling of jealousy, and actually shed a few tears for the simple reason Jason Leonard had taken the opportunity to make amends for the 1991 result, something he couldn't do. To put Leonard's longevity into perspective, I recall a conversation I was having with him concerning an international match he'd played early in his career when a certain Jonny Wilkinson, who was nearby, said, 'I remember that match, I was playing for Guildford Under 9s at the time.'

The Agony and the Ecstasy

Michael Lynagh

‘Michael represented Australia in seventy-two Test matches from 1984 to 1995 and held the world points-scoring record when he retired with a total of 911. He also played three seasons of club rugby in the UK with Saracens from 1996 to 1998. He was the first major signing after Nigel Wray took control of the club and his name attracted many overseas stars to join him at Sarries as well as a legion of new supporters.

‘It was during his time at Saracens when I got to know him best and found him to be a top man both on and off the pitch. As a fly-half with a considerable (and deserved) reputation, I have fond

memories of trying to flatten him during the matches we played against each other. Sadly he has more memories of successfully sidestepping, leaving me with a desperate expression on my face as I grasped fresh air.

'Most players in the world of international rugby have a few fans and the occasional detractor; in all the years I've known "Noddy" I've not heard a bad word said about him. He was a master at controlling a match and always seemed to find the time to talk to supporters from both teams after a game.

'He is still seen regularly on our television screens as an analyst for Sky Sports, a role he approaches in the same calm and measured way he approaches life. Having played in the first three World Cups he is more than qualified to provide a memory or two for this book. Here he provides first his thoughts on the 1987 tournament and then how he, sort of, captained his country to victory in 1991. I'm guessing he prefers the second one.'

Whatever Will Be, Will Be, We're Going to Rotorua . . .

I now live in the UK and see a few of my rugby contemporaries on a fairly regular basis. Occasionally the conversation will turn to the first World Cup in 1987 and many of the guys from the Home Nations tell me how it was a trip into the unknown, like a tour with no fixed return date. Although New Zealand was principal host, we played all our pool games, quarter-final and semi-final in Australia, travelling between Sydney and Brisbane. In fact many of the guys from Queensland and New South Wales would work in the mornings and then turn up for training in the afternoon with the rest of the squad. Most of these guys were also living at home while the rest of us were kicking our heels in the team hotel, waiting for their daily arrival. It was a very strange situation, some of us were 'on tour' in our own country, with the remainder working full time in their normal jobs and dropping in for training sessions whenever work permitted. Whilst not ideal preparation, particularly when compared with the modern era, we still felt we were in with a great chance of winning the tournament.

We progressed through the pool games with wins over England, the USA and Japan which ensured we topped our pool, securing a quarter-final against Ireland at the Concord Oval, Sydney. We felt in great shape and were determined to get to the final match of the tournament, at Eden Park, Auckland. If we achieved our ambition it would allow the entire squad to be together for an extended period of time rather than a couple of hours each afternoon. With a 33–15 victory over Ireland we were one match away from competing for the biggest prize in our sport.

In the semi-final we faced France, with 20,000 of our supporters drowning out the party of twenty-three travelling French fans. We were a 'shoo in' to get the trip to New Zealand. Unfortunately the French try scorers that day, Alain Lorieux, Philippe Sella, Patrice Lagisquet and the incomparable Serge Blanco, thought otherwise, and together with the on-form French goal-kicker Didier Camberabero they beat us 30–24.

The mood in our changing room was desperate, players sitting around in various states of undress, many of them holding their heads in their hands, staring at the floor. Even our flamboyant winger David Campese was unusually quiet. With the players desolate, I remember our coach Alan Jones entering the room to be greeted by the deafening silence. He wandered around, patted a few players on the back and checked on the welfare of guys who'd received knocks during the match. After several minutes he stood in the middle, surrounded by pieces of discarded kit and bandages, and said, 'Will someone at least turn on the bloody showers so we can create some atmosphere in here?' With the benefit of hindsight it was quite a good line, but it had no noticeable effect on the mood of the players, a mood which worsened when he informed us we were going to New Zealand after all, to compete in the third- and fourth-place playoff match in Rotorua, against either New Zealand or Wales, who were playing their semi-final the following day.

I don't want to cause any offence to Kiwis, particularly those who live in Rotorua, but I think it's fair to say that we weren't all that keen to travel there for a consolation match against Wales after such a disappointing loss. We arrived as a complete squad, took part in a few days' training and did what we could to raise ourselves for the non-match. We ran onto the pitch and were confronted by 20,000 screaming New Zealand Maoris, all supporting Wales and doing a comprehensive job of drowning out our dozen or so travelling fans. Eighty minutes later, following a last-minute touchline conversion from Welsh full-back Paul Thorburn, we were officially the fourth-best team in the world.

Acting the Part

The second Rugby World Cup four years later was a far more pleasurable experience for the Australian team and our supporters. Most of the bar staff, and 90 per cent of the transitory Aussie community in Earls Court, witnessed our victory over England at Twickenham, in addition to millions back home who set their alarms and watched it on TV at some unearthly hour. Several members of the squad had been playing back in the 1987 tournament and still carried the scars following the fourth-place finish. We were much better prepared than previously, not least because England is 12,000 miles away from Australia, thereby precluding any members of the squad from working at their day jobs during the tournament.

I suppose the game most people who follow rugby reasonably closely remember was our quarter-final against Ireland at Lansdowne Road, Dublin. This was a game we almost lost having never been behind until the seventy-sixth minute, when the Irish flanker Gordon Hamilton made a superb break from a line-out to score what thousands of Irish fans thought was the winning try. Robert Armstrong of the *Guardian* wrote, 'Australia and Ireland put on an enthralling exhibition of ambitious, freewheeling football in their quarter-final to leave Lansdowne Road in a state of high emotion. It was a classic demonstration of how fiercely committed underdogs can compel a favoured team to sweat every inch of the way for survival.'

This was an accurate reflection of the game. We were the favourites but at no point in the match were we comfortable until the final whistle blew with us leading 19–18. Of course when you get into the changing room things are completely different, cries of 'never in doubt' and 'all in a day's work' could be heard from various quarters (Campese predominantly). With Nick Farr-Jones aggravating a knee ligament injury early in the first half I had become acting captain for the remainder of the match, a responsibility I took seriously. With a semi-final to look forward to I wandered around the changing room having a word with a few players, letting them know how well I thought they'd done and congratulating them on not giving up. A future Australian captain who would lift the World Cup eight years later was a young member of the team that day, by the name of John Eales. I sat beside John and offered a few words of encouragement to the youngster. He was so wrapped up in his own thoughts it seemed as though he hadn't heard a word I'd said. I gave him a nudge and asked if he was okay. He turned, smiled at me and said, 'I am now we've won.' In that instant I realised how important it was to him to succeed. I can't say I knew he would become a future captain, but to me, in those few succinct words, he demonstrated the desire and passion required to play international rugby. He was going to be special, I was convinced.

'I was so worried with a few minutes to go when we went behind,' he continued. 'All I could think about was flying back to Australia tomorrow, and wondering how on earth I was going to get my dry cleaning which I put into the hotel laundry this morning. Do you think they would have posted it to me?'

I became acting captain once more during the tournament. It was at the official dinner following the final (in which we beat England, sorry Lol) held at the Lancaster Gate Hotel. Typically, it was a male-only affair, with about eight hundred people attending, at which various 'stuffed shirts' delivered proclamations about 'rugby football being the winner' and 'how wonderful the tournament had been in spreading the rugby union message to the world'. I'm a relatively quiet guy and I remember thinking how pleased I was not to have to make a speech that evening, or any other evening. I was happy doing what I needed to do on the pitch and then flying under the radar the rest of the time. By 10.00 p.m. I was pretty 'relaxed' and had just ordered a glass of port and my annual cigar, and was having a few quiet reflective moments before leaving the function, getting shot of the formal outfits and seriously getting stuck in back at the team hotel in Surrey. It was at this moment Nick Farr-Jones came up to me and said, 'I'm not feeling well, you're going to have to make the captain's speech on my behalf.' I could tell by the look on his face he was being serious and any doubts I might have had were dispelled as I saw him leave the room seconds later as a glass from the top table was being tapped with a knife to get everyone's attention.

Will Carling, the England captain, was invited to say a few words, none of which I heard as I was in a state of blind panic. What could I say? How should I pitch it? I didn't want to appear arrogant, but at the same time I wanted to recognise the huge achievement of winning the World Cup. I was in pieces as 'Nick Farr-Jones, captain of the Australian team' was invited to respond by Tony O'Reilly, the former Irish international and one of the best raconteurs I'd ever heard. It was only as I walked towards the microphone that suddenly I realised I was in the shoes everyone in that room wanted to be in; I was captain (okay, acting) of a World Cup-winning team. What a marvellous feeling, and once I had it in my mind I became instantly at ease. I have no recollection of what I said apart from thanking all the relevant personnel involved with the tournament in general and Australian rugby specifically. I'd like to think I did a reasonable job, and achieved a suitable balance between humility and pride in our achievement.

This may sound immodest, but I think Nick Farr-Jones did well in choosing me as his deputy that night. Another option would have been David Campese, and had Nick gone down that route it's quite possible the dinner might still have been going on now.

Double Victory

Sean Fitzpatrick

‘During an international career lasting twelve years, Sean played in ninety-two Test matches for New Zealand as hooker, and captained the team from 1992 until his retirement in 1997. As a player he was absolutely fearless and never gave up, and in many respects he epitomises the ethos of All Black rugby. I remember hearing him speak at a function a few years ago and a couple of things from his talk remain with me. When discussing the All Black philosophy he said that when your opposite number comes up to you at the end of a game and asks if you want to swap your jersey, "Ask yourself, does he deserve it?" The other thing which struck a chord was in a changing room following a defeat, when the captain of New Zealand told his team to

"Remember this feeling, remember how you feel right now, and know you never want to feel this way again. We celebrate our victories and remember our defeats."

'When listening to some of the platitudes spoken by players from losing teams saying "we'll learn from this and move on" or "we'll put this behind us" it made me realise how much sense there is in the All Black approach.

'Sean has lived in the UK for many years and whenever we meet, which is fairly often, we always enjoy a couple of beers and a bit of reminiscing about how good we used to be.

'In 1997 Sean was awarded the New Zealand Order of Merit by the then Governor General of New Zealand, Sir Michael Hardie Boys. He remains an icon in New Zealand and is highly respected throughout the rugby world.'

I remember looking forward to the 1991 Rugby World Cup with a huge amount of anticipation. Firstly, we entered the tournament as defending champions (a situation we haven't found ourselves in since) and secondly, it provided us with the opportunity to prove conclusively we were the best team in the world by following up our home victory with a win on foreign soil, and in the northern hemisphere. It was a challenge I relished, as was the chance to compete against the English hooker Brian Moore.

The opening game of the 1991 World Cup was England against New Zealand at Twickenham. It was the occasion of my thirty-fifth Test match and marked the first time I ever played against Brian. Obviously I'd heard a lot about him and knew he enjoyed making comments to the press which were often designed to wind up the opposition, a tactic which proved particularly successful when playing against France and Scotland I believe.

The first time I saw him was while we were performing the haka a few minutes before kick-off. He was smaller than I'd imagined and not exactly the most handsome hooker I'd ever faced. Now I don't want to give the wrong impression here. I didn't generally judge hookers by their looks, but there was something about Brian that stood out. Or rather didn't. It was his lack of a full set of teeth that caught my eye. In some individuals, the look can indicate a degree of meanness and aggression, but to me it always says a guy who was just too slow to get his face out of the way. I wasn't sure if he smiled or snarled when he caught my eye, but he certainly made an impression. Apparently there is an explanation for his absent dentures. It seems he fell asleep as a child with his head under the pillow and later that night the tooth fairy arrived and took the lot. At this early stage in the story you may be thinking I'm being a bit harsh on Brian, but believe me he deserves it.

Sledging has been an integral part of cricket for generations. There are legendary tales of players verbally attacking each other in order to gain some kind of psychological advantage. Rugby has always been much simpler in its approach to intimidation. If you want to send someone a message, punch them! It was during the match in 1991 that I first witnessed sledging from a rugby player, and there are no prizes for guessing that the sledger was Brian Moore and the recipient was me. In fact, the sledging was completely unnecessary as he'd already caught me off guard with a sneaky jab to my jaw. That was fine. If you play the game of rugby you know at some point or another someone is going to send a punch in your direction. In Brian's case I think I annoyed him during the first scrum when our 'baby faces' came into contact and I muttered something about not understanding how he had the nickname 'The Pitbull' when surely it would have been more appropriate to be called 'ugly duckling'. He bided his time and shortly before half-time landed the shot I mentioned earlier. I heard a couple of gasps from the English forwards, clearly not surprised Brian had lost his cool, but worried they might be required to back him up if I decided to retaliate. To be fair to Brian he had done what he felt he had to and even more importantly had managed to do it without alerting the referee. He should have left it there, but instead, he leant forward as I was clearing my head and said in a loud, excited voice, 'And I slept with your mother last night.'

I have to be honest, the comment briefly stopped the game as everyone contemplated the words he'd shouted at me. And I was slightly perturbed. Mum had been in London the previous night.

By now everyone was staring at me including the referee. Was I going to ignore the comment? Or was I going to erupt? It was before the days of red and yellow cards but the ref was definitely reaching in his pocket for something, probably his whistle so he could give it a loud blast in an attempt to assert his authority before I whacked Brian. He needn't have worried. Me? A hothead? Never. Instead, in a very calm voice I said, 'Brian, you're twenty-nine years of age, my mother is sixty-two. By my reckoning that's a result for Mum.'

Match result – New Zealand 18 England 12

Personal result – Sean Fitzpatrick 1 Brian Moore 0

On the Edge

Will Carling

'Prior to Will Carling, England captains remained relatively anonymous outside of the Five Nations Championship. His time in charge coincided with a period of success and a greater media interest in the sport which thrust him into the spotlight. He became the youngest post-War England captain aged twenty-two and led the team to back-to-back Grand Slams in 1991 and 1992. He gained seventy-two England caps, no fewer than fifty-nine as captain. He also toured with the British and Irish Lions to New Zealand in 1993.

'While the style of play adopted under his leadership was often criticised as being dominated by the forwards, it was successful and rare victories over Australia, South Africa and New Zealand saw a huge rise in the sport's popularity in England and across the Home Nations.

'Just prior to the 1995 World Cup Will was famously relieved of the captaincy for referring to the Rugby Football Union Committee as "fifty-seven old farts", a comment made in reaction to their pronouncement that England players had a desire to "cheat" by breaking the amateur ethics of the game (the comment was not meant for public consumption as he believed the interview was over and the microphones turned off, something former Prime Minister Gordon Brown thought during last year's election campaign I believe). He was, however, soon reinstated following a public show of support and a personal apology. Just a few months later the game became professional.

'There is no doubt Will and his team raised the profile of the sport and his centre partnership with Jerry Guscott was the most successful English pairing for several generations.'

International teams are always looking to find an edge over the opposition. Obviously in recent years the search for any such advantage has become increasingly high-tech, and some of the gadgetry around now would not be out of place in a Hollywood blockbuster. For several years there have been devices available that measure a player's heart-rate, the total distance run and top speed. These were in their infancy when I was involved in the sport and most of the players treated them with a degree of scepticism. Results were often read out in team meetings prior to going out on the pitch to train.

Inevitably Peter Winterbottom, our world-class open-side flanker, would run in excess of twelve miles during a match, stopping only to add his weight to a scrum or assist in a line-out, and even then he was often seen running on the spot. Someone like Jason Leonard, however, would never break the six-mile-an-hour barrier, but to be honest I never cared about his speed (or lack of it) because I knew the damage he could inflict on opposition scrums and was well aware of his value at rucks and mauls (those he managed to get to anyway). But the statistics did sometimes reveal interesting facts. For instance, we discovered that the quickest player in the squad was our 'flying winger' Rory Underwood. Hardly a surprise you would think, considering he played eight-five times for England and scored a record forty-nine tries. Swerving to evade a sprawling defender would surely be the moment when his foot slammed down on the accelerator to achieve maximum acceleration, one would imagine. Ah, not so, I am afraid to report. Rory was clocked in full flight as he ran in celebration towards Jerry Guscott, who had just scored a try. You have to take your hat off to a guy whose top speed during eighty minutes was reached in order to give a team-mate a hug!

Today, the devices are far more advanced, data is fed via a small transmitter in a player's collar to a laptop computer in the stands, recording such things as an individual's core temperature, and even the level of fatigue they are experiencing. This information will then assist a coach when deciding whether or not it's the right time to make a substitution. In my day the players were pretty good at making these decisions themselves. I can recall various occasions when Wade Dooley looked at me gasping, 'Will, I'm f****** hot and feel shagged out. Either go down injured to give me a rest or get someone else on.' I can't help thinking it was more personal during my time.

With little relevant technology in 1991, management teams were much less sophisticated when it came to finding the edge. Following the group stages of the World Cup, our team manager Geoff Cooke decided we needed a bit of rest and recreation prior to our quarter-final in Paris against France. He arranged for a two-day trip to Jersey which included players' wives and girlfriends (I can't remember any player inviting both). R & R, that was all we needed to gain the edge. On the first night all the playing members of the squad and their partners were having a meal in the hotel and Brian Moore, our hooker, resident commercial lawyer and viticulture connoisseur, was placed in charge of ordering the wine. With his extensive knowledge – he could tell white from red, providing he had his eyes open – he did what any one of us would have done in the same situation. He studied the right-hand side of the list and ordered numerous bottles of the most expensive white, red and rosé wines available. He succeeded in running up a bill of over £5,000, ensuring the R & R session developed into a superb team bonding exercise. I even have a vague recollection of one of the forwards telling one of the backs that he loved him. Talking of forwards, the aforementioned super-fit Peter Winterbottom was even seen dancing 'cowboy style' on a makeshift dance floor. To understand the enormity of this you need to know that Winters was a man of very few words and (until that moment) even fewer dance moves.

A couple of days later we went for a team run before departing for the airport. I was ambling along doing a good captain's job, forcing myself to stay at the back to be able to encourage some of the slower forwards, when on my right-hand side I heard the voice of Winters saying, 'Sorry, mate.' I looked in his direction and asked what he was apologising for. 'The other night. Sorry, mate, I let myself down, sorry, it won't happen again.' With that he ran off and took up his customary position at the front of the group. Those few words were more than he said to me throughout the rest of the campaign and probably to anyone else as well, but it made me realise how important the break had been in recharging the batteries and getting away from rugby just for a short while. It might not have been sophisticated but it gave us an edge.

We went on to win the quarter-final and semi-final and I feel certain if we'd had another Jersey visit before the final we might well have won that as well. Never underestimate the importance of a bit of R & R and a man who knows his way around a wine list.

Four years later and the World Cup had moved to South Africa. The tournament was bigger, as were the squads and management teams. On numerous occasions we'd be out on the park training and I'd look at the touchline thinking to myself, who on earth are all these people in England tracksuits? We had dieticians, physiotherapists, doctors, forwards coaches, backs coaches, liaison officers, press officers; we even had an entertainments officer. I'm sure they all had important roles to play, and as it happens none more so than Dr Austin Swain, the team psychologist.

Once again we'd progressed through the group stages and were preparing for a quarter-final against Australia. What could we do to gain an advantage over our opposition? We knew where the Aussies were staying and where they trained. We also knew, having spent a few weeks together before and during the World Cup, that Dr Austin Swain could do a more than passable Australian accent. In addition, he had been underused in his official capacity as several members of the squad did not understand the benefits sports psychology could bring to them as individuals and the team in general. No matter how often I tried to explain, a few of the boys kept telling me that they had no need to get the Ouija board out to contact the other side. 'Listen lads, he's not a psychic, he's a . . . oh, never mind.' So we decided to send him to an Australian training session disguised as an Aussie backpacker to see what information he could glean. For the record, despite the sceptics, Dr Austin Swain made a valuable contribution to our mental preparation.

Several hours later he returned having bluffed his way into their session, saying something about 'a sporting thesis incorporating the mental and physical preparation required at elite level' (like he was ever going to find out anything on that topic from the Aussies!). Not only had they given him a few isotonic drinks during training, they had also sent him on his way with a couple of six-packs of beer. What they didn't know was he also left with full details and diagrams on all their attacking moves and defensive strategies which allowed us the best part of a week to come up with counter-measures. Although it was a close match we finished victorious after a period of extra-time (we had 'the edge').

Our prize for winning that match came seven days later, when the whistle blew to start our semi-final match against New Zealand and we were introduced to a lad called Jonah Lomu. Need I say more?

Maybe justice was not just seen to be done, it was done.

The Tipping Pint

Philip Matthews

‘Philip was an uncompromising Irish back-row forward who played thirty-eight times for his country, thirteen as captain. Interestingly, he is one of a small group of players who have played for the British and Irish Lions in a “home” fixture, when they played France as part of the bicentennial celebrations of the French Revolution in 1989. He also has the distinction of appearing on two postage stamps, one issued by Tadjikistan after the 1991 Rugby World Cup, where he is depicted tackling Australian fly-half Michael Lynagh, and the other by the Republic of Turkmenistan, on which he is facing the Australian team in the same tournament. Fame indeed. Currently Philip is the eighth President of the National College of Ireland,

a position he took up in February 2010, and I am assuming there won't be a third stamp in the offing, featuring him at his desk. But you never know, I guess.

'Phil had the reputation of giving 100 per cent on the field of play and 100 per cent off it. If there was a tackle to be made you could rely on him to make it, conversely if there was a beer to be drunk it more often than not had his name on it. Many people will recognise Phil today as the touchline analyst during international matches featuring Ireland at Lansdowne Road. Here he gives us a fascinating insight into how different the teams' approach in the second World Cup was compared with the first.'

I was fortunate to play in two World Cup competitions, the inaugural event in 1987 and again in 1991, and my overriding memory is how markedly different from each other they were. I'm not talking about the obvious: the first being in the southern hemisphere and the second in the northern hemisphere. To me the most marked difference was the approach of the teams and the attitude of the players.

In 1987 one team stood apart from all the rest, the All Blacks. They had been a professional outfit for many years (professional in their approach is of course what I mean) and were generally regarded as the best team in the world at the time, something they were to prove on 20 June 1987 when they swept France aside 29–9 in the final in Auckland. The other nations were either several steps behind or there simply to make up the numbers; New Zealand were always going to win that first World Cup.

The Home Nations didn't really view it as a competition, more like a tour, the only difference being the more successful you were the longer you got to have fun. I should explain, these were the great amateur days of rugby union and in addition to the Five Nations Championship, most teams enjoyed an international tour every couple of years. If you were really lucky, your union would choose a destination like the USA, Fiji, Japan or Tonga where the standard of rugby at the time was limited but the hospitality fantastic. Less fortunate were those who toured Australia or New Zealand, and when I say less fortunate I mean on the rugby front because you knew even at provincial level you were not going to get an easy ride on the field. Still, wherever you went the hospitality remained excellent and there was always plenty of time away from the practice field when the boys could 'relax'.

This tour mentality was firmly in place when we arrived in Wellington for the opening pool game against Wales. You may be interested to know we also shared the same hotel as Wales leading up to this fixture. In the modern era, hotels are researched and booked often years in advance, to ensure everything is 'just right'. It is inconceivable two teams would share the same hotel, and certainly not two teams who were playing against each other. Actually for the Irish lads this was quite normal, as for many years all visiting teams to Dublin used to stay in the

Shelbourne Hotel with the Irish team, to help negate any possible threat from the IRA.

We had a few (very few) days to get over jetlag, and trained for a couple of hours on each of these days. To be honest even without jetlag we only used to train for a couple of hours a day, leaving twenty-two other ones in which to get up to mischief. We were not very creative when it came to organising our downtime, in fact a trip to the nearest watering hole tended to be the height of our ambitions. Unsurprisingly Wales followed a very similar routine and we often found ourselves sharing the same bar as well as the same hotel. Obviously many of the players from the respective teams knew each other, but for others it was a chance to get to know some of the opposition as well as forging stronger links with their own team-mates. It was all an essential element of our meticulous preparations, we told ourselves, as we ordered yet another round.

I remember spending one evening having a 'couple' of drinks with a few of the Welsh lads, including the winger Glen Webbe. Glen was twenty-five years of age and having made his debut for Wales the year before was on his first overseas trip representing his country. He was definitely making the most of it, often leaving the bar at closing time to visit nightclubs in search of some 'action'. If the truth be told he was often seen on these occasions dancing with himself, but always with a smile on his face. He was definitely a lively lad who no doubt helped to raise the spirits of the Welsh side when required. This particular evening he was exceptionally good company and summed up his approach, and probably that of most of the teams, as he said, 'When I die I don't want to go to heaven; I want to go on tour.' Hallelujah, brother! To a man we all agreed with that sentiment.

So with most teams lacking either ability or application, the All Blacks showed the world how far advanced they were in all aspects of the game. At the time I remember thinking they would win every World Cup for generations to come, but as we all know that has not been the case, although I think this may change this year when the tournament returns to New Zealand.

The manner of the All Black victory was a much-needed kick up the arse to the sport in general. Even those who wished it wasn't so recognised that rugby had to change, and in the interim period between World Cups all the serious nations made radical improvements in their approach to the game. Rather than treat everyone the same, coaches were utilised to prepare units within the team, so the 'flying wingers' no longer did the same physical training as the prop forwards. This was of massive benefit to both sets of players. Everything became more specialised; nutritionists were brought in to give players advice on diet, and it wasn't just whether salt 'n' vinegar or cheese 'n' onion went better with a pint of the black stuff (to be fair not everyone accepted the advice, but at least they had the information). Some nations even employed the services of sports psychologists to train the top three inches (the brain). That proved trickier than anticipated for some of my team-mates, and on occasion the experts had to settle for the top inch. It was all they could find.

I suppose the reality is everything continues to move on and although we felt we were at the cutting edge then, what we were doing in the late eighties and early nineties would be laughed at today.

Humorous stories from the world of rugby have historically often involved alcohol to a greater or lesser extent. I have no recollection of 'big nights out' in the 1991 World Cup, whilst 1987 was full of them. The pints had been spilled for good. We were no longer on tour, we were in competition.

The lead-up to 1991 was especially poor for Ireland. We didn't win a match in the Five Nations Championship that year, although we did manage a draw against Wales. We were also beaten by the rugby minnows Namibia and by the club side Gloucester in our World Cup warm-up matches. However, when the tournament actually arrived we were so much better prepared than four years earlier.

We played against Scotland in one of our pool games and I remember Finlay Calder, the Scottish back-row forward, 'taking out' our full-back Jim Staples with a thundering tackle, which in truth was only slightly late. Jim definitely had a touch of concussion and Gary Armstrong, the Scottish scrum-half, could see Jim was not quite all there. From the next scrum Armstrong hoisted a huge high ball which Jim failed to gather and Scotland scored from the resulting fumble. At the time I remember thinking how sharp it was from Scotland's perspective. They had seen a weakness and immediately exploited it. They too had learnt lessons from 1987 when witnessing first-hand the clinical approach of New Zealand in that tournament.

For the Irish our big day was the quarter-final against Australia at Lansdowne Road. The match will remain with me for ever and lives as a reminder of the validity of the saying, 'It's not over until the fat lady sings.' With five minutes left on the clock we were losing 15–12, when the ball popped into the hands of our open-side flanker Gordon Hamilton, who stormed past Australian winger David Campese, leaving him completely for dead as he sprinted forty yards to score (at least that's how

Gordon remembers it). He was mobbed by his team-mates, including myself and a host of spectators. We thought we had qualified for the semi-finals, especially when the reliable Ralph Keyes slotted home the conversion for an additional two points, taking us into a three-point lead. With seconds remaining we conceded a penalty and the Australian genius at outside half Michael Lynagh looked as though he was going to take a kick at goal which if successful would have drawn the game.

Instead of the kick he took a quick tap penalty which stunned the Irish defence who started to rush around trying to close all the gaps. Australian backs Tim Horan and Jason Little both made valuable ground before passing the ball to Campese, who was tackled literally inches from the Irish try line. As he hit the ground he popped the ball up to Lynagh who bounced over the line to score. Within a minute the Irish supporters and players had gone from absolute elation to heartbreak as we lost 19–18 and were out of the tournament. Australia went on to win the World Cup a couple of weeks later when they defeated England in the final – we were so close. We had made significant strides forward, that was true, but they were clearly not quite long enough.

The beginning of the end of rugby as it should be played, or a long overdue catalyst for change, however you want to see it, the 1987 Rugby World Cup was a game-changer. The tipping point, if you like. The preparation of teams and the sharpness of players have been on a continuous upward curve since that tournament, whereas for generations prior to 1987 little happened to threaten the status quo. I know from personal experience we were much more organised and professional in our approach to 1991 and it's clear to see the standard of world rugby has continued to improve since then. Has this benefited the sport I love? Well, I'll leave you with the thought that since 1987, to play in a Rugby World Cup is the ambition of almost every serious player, and to watch one is a joy for supporters around the globe.

Zut Alors!

Alan Whetton

‘One of the big names in All Black history, Alan gained thirty-five caps and scored forty points in his Test career. He is the twin brother of Gary Whetton, who also played for New Zealand in fifty-eight Tests.

‘In his early career he played No. 8 and second row, before establishing himself as blind-side flanker. It was in this position he became part of the formidable back-row trio which included Michael Jones and Wayne (“Buck”) Shelford, who together played an integral part in the All Blacks’ success in the 1987 tournament. He remained an influential member of the team until their semi-final defeat to arch-rivals Australia four years later. Following his retirement from the international scene he

became player-coach at Kobe Steel in Japan from 1996 to 1999, before returning to New Zealand where he was a commentator for New Zealand's TV3 network during their coverage of the 2007 RWC. He was also part of the Solid Gold (radio) breakfast team for several years. Alan is an eloquent man who displays in the story below the ability to talk his way out of a potentially sticky situation during his playing days.'

It has long been said every male born in New Zealand wants to be an All Black, and having lived there for the majority of my life I can tell you it's not far from the truth. This makes playing for the national team even more special when you finally get selected, knowing it's the dream of at least half the nation. There are, however, one or two misconceptions about the New Zealand All Blacks, one of which is we never celebrate victory (apart from a World Cup final win and, as everyone involved in rugby outside New Zealand constantly reminds me, that's not happened for a long time).

We are no different in this respect from all the other rugby-playing nations around the world: we go out and have a few beers, occasionally too many beers, and then get back to training and preparation for the next match. Incidentally, it's worth mentioning that the philosophy of All Black rugby since inception has been to win the next match and for the best part of one hundred years this served us well, up to and including the inaugural World Cup in 1987. Following our victory then it was felt we needed to change, as it was clear the sport's landscape had altered for ever. Winning the Webb Ellis Cup was now the dominant factor in the eyes of everyone involved in world rugby and so although we still went out to win every game, we were also planning up to four years ahead. This meant at certain times we were not picking the best team. The reason being, coaches and selectors would look at a player who was perhaps turning thirty years of age two or three years prior to a World Cup and make the decision that he would not be around for the tournament. A new younger player, possibly not as good as the incumbent at that moment, would then be drafted into the side. This happened many times and numerous players had their international careers cut prematurely short. I believe now we have gone back to our roots by once again always targeting the next game – we shall see in 2011 if it has paid off!

Anyway back to All Black celebrations. In 1991 we played a quarter-final match against Canada, on paper a relatively easy and not too abrasive match for us. But as we all know, matches are not played on paper and the Canadians had clearly decided they were going to make history by beating us and reaching the semi-finals. It was a brutally tough match and the final score of 29–13 in our favour was flattering. I'm not saying we deserved to lose, but they were much closer to us than that score suggests.

Following the match, which was an evening kick-off in Lille (about seventy miles from Calais), we had a quick court session to pass sentence on all the player misdemeanours brought to the attention of the 'judge', which happened to me on this occasion.

I was particularly harsh on all the miscreants, while at the same time being sure to keep the non-offenders drinking steadily throughout the proceedings. Once the final sentence had been handed down the majority of us went to our rooms and changed into our drinking gear, which consisted of casual clothes and an All Blacks blazer. This latter item was essential as it seemed to contain certain magical properties which meant queues at busy bars and clubs would miraculously disappear as we approached. Very handy.

It was now around midnight and several of us were outside the team hotel waiting for a taxi to take us into town. Unfortunately there were also about a hundred other residents milling around with the same idea in mind, and not even the blazer was going to get us to the front of that queue. I won't name the other guys but I was certainly one of those who spotted a maintenance van to the right of the main entrance. We'd seen these vans from time to time during our stay and they'd always been parked at the rear of the hotel. This one was obviously on a flying visit to either drop off or pick something up, because as we approached the little Citroën we noticed the engine was running, and on closer inspection it was empty apart from a dog in the back.

Seeing an opportunity, four or five of us piled into the van. I made sure to sit in the passenger seat, only to be confronted by a steering wheel. I had forgotten that while we have right-hand drive in New Zealand, France clearly doesn't. By default I was therefore on driving duty, so as the boys in the back introduced themselves to the dog, off I sped into the night. A few minutes later we pulled up outside a nightclub. I asked the doorman to look after the vehicle for us and showed him the dog in the back, explaining in my pidgin French, reinforced by hand gestures and vivid facial expressions, that it was a ferocious guard dog that should not be approached under any circumstances. We entered the club and continued our celebrations, oblivious to the phone call being made from the owner of the van reporting it stolen to the local gendarmerie.

It would seem they had put the great French detective Inspector Clouseau on the case, as it took almost two hours before the doorman approached me inside the bar to explain the arrival of the gendarmes, accompanied by flashing lights and sirens, and their desire to have a word. As my fingerprints were on the steering wheel my fellow team-mates generously decided I should go out and face the wrath of the local police while they continued their celebrations. I exited into the cold night air and instantly realised this was potentially very serious. It is hard to miss three police cars and a riot van all on full alert. After a cordial discussion, a lift back to the hotel and a generous distribution of All Black ties, shirts, training kit and some silver ferns, we were released from their custody with a stern warning and a slap on the wrists.

Thinking back, I was an All Black playing in a World Cup, drunk whilst driving a stolen vehicle in a foreign country, obviously with no insurance – and a kidnapped dog. I was extremely lucky, and am certain that if the events of that night had occurred in the professional era I would have been front-page news, my international career over and facing a probable jail sentence. I noticed last year that the Welsh back row forward Andy Powell celebrated their last-minute win over Scotland in the Six Nations Championship by driving a golf buggy (on a motorway, mind you) whilst intoxicated and was fined £1,000 and handed a fifteen-month driving ban. On reading the news report I gave thanks for the leniency and understanding of the French police back in 1991.

This is just one instance of All Black celebration; believe me there were many more and they still go on today, although the current squad are probably not quite as stupid as I was in my playing days. Or perhaps they're just more discreet?

Collective Responsibility

Simon Halliday

'Simon was a product of Oxford University where he achieved Blues in both rugby and cricket. In fact he scored a first-class century (113 not out) against Kent in 1982. He played twenty-three times for England from 1986 to 1992. Many people feared he would not play top-flight rugby following a serious break and dislocation of his ankle when playing for Somerset against Middlesex in 1983. However, twelve months of intensive rehabilitation, coupled with his immense personal drive, saw him return to his club side Bath and go on to play in five successful Cup finals at Twickenham, before moving to Harlequins and pursuing a career as a merchant

banker in the City at the end of the decade. He played predominantly in the centre, but with Carling and Guscott occupying those berths in 1991 he gained a place on the wing during the World Cup tournament.

'You will have recognised by now, most players I asked to contribute World Cup memories or stories have proceeded down the humorous or heartfelt route. Having read Simon's valued contribution, he clearly wanted to vent his frustration following twenty years of pain since England's defeat in the 1991 final. I'm glad this book has been of some assistance in his "anger therapy".'

Who could ever forget that wet November 2003 evening in Sydney, when England's rugby team became champions of the world? People who were there still describe it as the top sporting event of their lives. When it comes to achievement at the highest levels of sport, 2003's victory is up there with the best of them – Alf Ramsey and the boys of 1966, Steve Redgrave's haul of Olympic gold medals, the odd Ashes series victory, in 1981 or again in 2005.

Frustratingly I was stuck in my City office that week in 2003, but I watched the match at home with a select gathering, my son Alexander, my godson Matthew Luddington and his father Richard. It was fantastic to see the looks on the boys' faces at the moment they will always remember, when their hero Jonny Wilkinson landed the winning dropped goal.

Text messages came through thick and fast from mates of mine who were in the stadium, and later on I had a few words with Andy Robinson, who berated me for not being there. He briefly described the scene: 'Here I am at Manly Beach, which is covered with drunken English rugby supporters either in the surf or barbecuing. What a sight!' I was mildly gutted, to say the least.

Those were moments of a lifetime, and brought back memories of a similarly cold November day in 1991 when I was a member of another England team contesting a World Cup final against Australia. Most of my City clients were there, as were work colleagues, one of them in fact acting as a steward for the day, dressed up in fluorescent yellow and marshalling the crowds. He was doing it purely out of the goodness of his heart and certainly not because he had failed to get a ticket!

Despite a valiant effort England just failed to conquer possibly the best Australian team ever to take the field, boasting the likes of David Campese, Nick Farr-Jones, Michael Lynagh, Tim Horan and Jason Little. Not a bad quintet for starters. That said, there is no excuse for losing a game we should have won. The Australian changing room in the immediate aftermath resembled the finishing line of a marathon, with players strewn across the floor in states of exhaustion. Notwithstanding the cynical play of Campese, when he seemed to deliberately knock the ball on to prevent us from scoring, the game had been a heroic piece of Australian defence. They grabbed an early lead, and then simply hung on. Farr-Jones was their extra defender in the back line, instead of in his usual position around the fringes. He, like the rest of the world, spotted we were suddenly playing an expansive game, whereas in the lead-up to the tournament (away games in France and Scotland), and indeed in the 1991 Grand Slam season, England had played tight, controlled rugby. So why the big change? And did it account for our failure to go down in history?

Some well-known figures thought so. Brian Moore, Peter Winterbottom, Mike Teague and Jeff Probyn have all pointed the finger in their own way, criticising England's tactics. And I thought rugby was a team game. More importantly, all four of these English heroes were never short of a word on, or off, the pitch, and they had been an integral part of everything we had achieved. It was collective will which had taken us from being an under-achieving bunch of no-hopers to the crest of world domination.

Many years ago I remember reading a line from a sports book, the name of which sadly I cannot now remember so please accept my paraphrasing. 'The gap between accepting things the way they are and wishing them to be otherwise is the 1/10 of an inch of difference between heaven and hell.' Never were wiser words written.

The passing up of a great opportunity, on home ground, still feels unacceptable twenty years after the event. It is particularly hard to take when considering the incredible scenes of jubilation surrounding the 2003 triumph. In comparison, being described as a participant in the 1991 Rugby World Cup final reeks of failure. And of course that's what it was. But was all the criticism from within justified? Were all the senior players disenfranchised and as powerless to effect change as they have intimated? Were they victims of a conspiracy of events beyond their control and influence, such as having no 'plan B', Will Carling's leadership, intransigence, the half-backs not mixing the game up etc., etc.?

I hope my version of events may just clear up some points of 'confusion'. In the week leading up to the final, we had talked for hours about the best way to beat Australia, who had a near-perfect mix of youth and experience and were arguably more talented than us. It should be remembered we had played them in Sydney that July, and had been roundly beaten. I was on the bench that day, to see David Campese give Chris Oti the complete run-around. As a result the scoreline was one to make an Englishman wince, turning defeat into a rout. But the video showed England had cut open the Aussies whenever they moved the ball wide. Guscott, Webb and Underwood had all looked like world-beaters. Time and again the outside gaps appeared, whereas we were getting no reward from the exchanges up front.

It was this experience that caused Geoff Cooke and Roger Uttley, England team manager and coach respectively, to consider a tactical shift. I say 'shift' rather than 'revolution' because the previous year we were the most attractive side to watch in Europe, as demonstrated by the record away win in France and the record home win against Wales. We knew how to do it. The change in tactics was not an alien concept. It was just that throughout 1991 we had chosen to play tight rugby, with two big away games in the World Cup at hostile grounds not surprisingly keeping it that way in the campaign itself. But in the final the stakes were at a new high. Could we win a World Cup playing ten-man rugby? Everyone asked the same question, and the answer was no. So there we were: *Alea jacta est.* ('The die is cast', as Caesar said crossing the Rubicon, in case you were wondering.) We all bought into it, we practised it all week, and we went out to implement the agreed strategy. But we failed. Our execution was poor, and, incredibly, the passing of the ever-reliable Will

Carling and Jerry Guscott was just not good enough on the day. Rob Andrew and Richard Hill were seemingly bewildered by all the possession, so much so they forgot about flexibility. The back row played like headless chickens (I always thought Mick 'The Munch' Skinner had chicken legs), and had to take their share of the blame along with the half-backs. I felt sorry for the front five because they did all that was asked of them. They even ran about in the loose, a great sight, Paul Ackford and Wade Dooley on the rampage.

As for Australia? They played a blinder. John Eales, a second-row forward no less, caught Rob Andrew from behind in full flight. Rob was no Rory Underwood, but the adrenalin coursing through the young Aussie lock must have been incredible. Otherwise how else could he have done that? According to Jeff Probyn, Will Carling was urged to change tactics at half-time. Well, not in the game in which I was playing. I am not exonerating Will. He was the captain, and he could have shouted the odds at the most experienced English side ever to have taken the field. Perhaps it was a bridge too far for the twenty-five-year-old, who had melded together an improbable bunch of players into a great team? Maybe there was a lack of tactical experience in a man who had played just fifty to sixty first-class games in his entire career at that point, despite three years as England captain? But I would challenge anyone to have made themselves heard in the heat of this particular battle. My conclusion is that, no, it was not Will's fault. He had brought us to the brink of glory. It is said that a leader needs the wisdom to serve and follow, as well as to lead. On a day when none of us could hear each other speak, the self-appointed critics might do better to look within. We all participated in our defeat and individually contributed towards it.

What I do know is that it was the greatest rugby adventure, a glorious, typically English failure, but we were a world force, with a rightful place at the top table.

When the nation awoke on the Sunday, the reality was that we had fallen at the last hurdle to exorcise twenty-five years of English sporting underachievement since 1966. One client later revealed to me that in the aftermath of defeat he simply gazed at the ground, unable to speak. It meant that much to everyone, supporters and players alike, all left with a feeling just as empty as the Grand Slam defeat against Scotland the previous year.

My wife Suzanne and I returned to our Putney home, reunited with Sophie our two-year-old, me clutching a loser's medal. The story goes that Brian Moore threw his in the river in disgust – well, mine is framed on my bedroom wall. And why not? It was a monumental effort, and we had made a nation proud. I will celebrate that fact for ever and will never forget the crowd as we left the Rose Room at Twickenham to go to the post-match reception. There were hundreds of them waiting for us outside, and they broke into song as we boarded the bus. I recollect they gave us a rendition of 'Jerusalem'. Perhaps I am wrong, but it doesn't matter much. What does matter was that they were there, acknowledging our mutual disappointment and offering us all a sense of companionship. That is what sport is about and that is what should be remembered.

In the financial world, we discount events and move on. The entire game had been dissected by coffee time on the Monday morning – yet the impression of the tournament was long-lasting and indelible. Football-mad market-makers found their sons wanting to take up mini-rugby. The Five Nations tournament became a persistent topic, and days out to Paris, Dublin,

Edinburgh and Cardiff were feverishly planned. My 'team leader' took me into a meeting room to discuss my return to work. I was reasonably scared of him because he was bright, very demanding, and didn't tolerate fools. It came as a surprise, then, when he said, 'Take your time getting back into it. You must feel gutted, we all do. What a traumatic experience; don't worry if you don't feel like working.' I was nonplussed, and had no idea how to react. He was very emotional, and reality suddenly dawned on me. Even hardened City men realised we had been on the verge of something special and felt the disappointment themselves. My boss even suggested that I take another two weeks' holiday to recover. What, after twelve weeks away? My immediate colleagues would have been well impressed! I politely declined.

Not only had my long absence from the office failed to bring back the World Cup, it also provided an excuse to say I couldn't possibly expect a bonus having been away for so long. Fair, but still depressing, and it grated on me that I was losing out financially while playing to full houses all around the country. Nobody ever did the sums on how much revenue was being collected by the RFU. All I knew was that it certainly failed to come in the direction of the players.

That said, would I change a thing really? Yes, only the result. But I played for my country in a World Cup final. I am not going to gripe about that.

Friends in High Places

Tim Horan

‘Tim was consistently one of the best centres in world rugby throughout the nineties and is one of a small number of players to have won the World Cup twice, in 1991 and 1999. In fact he was voted Player of the Tournament in 1999, an award he combined with scoring the fastest try, which won him a year’s supply of Guinness. I can only think how thankful Guinness must have been to present the prize to Tim Horan and not Jason Leonard. Think of the damage it would have done to company profits if they had been obliged to supply twelve months at Jase’s rate of consumption. Mind you, I don’t think the shareholders would have been losing much sleep over the potential risk. The words “fastest” and “Jason Leonard” rarely come together. By the end of Tim's international career he had amassed eighty caps for Australia scoring 140 points.

'He made an impact from his very first game in 1989 against New Zealand, when he impressed his opposite number, Joe Stanley, so much that Stanley gave Tim his Test jersey and told him to keep his own as it was his first. In 1994 his career nearly ended with a horrific knee injury in the Super 10 final, which resulted in over a year of rehabilitation before making the squad for the 1995 World Cup defence in South Africa.

'I played many times against Tim at international level and also when he played club rugby for Saracens towards the end of his career. He never gave anything less than 100 per cent and always seemed to make the right decisions at the right time, in attack and defence. Off the field he displays modesty and humility and remains a real gentleman.

'Tim is currently a banker for Westpac Banking Corporation. He is an ambassador for the Spinal Injuries Association, speaking to school children regarding prevention of spinal injuries. In addition he is also an ambassador for Aunties and Uncles – a non-profit organisation offering friendship, role-modelling and support for children in single-parent

or parentless families. In 2009 he was made a Member of the Order of Australia.

I would like to start by paying a brief tribute to Lawrence, whom I played against on many occasions. For me Lawrence was the face of English rugby even when Martin Johnson captained the team, and for a number of years he was quite simply the best No. 8 in the world. [Ed note: Okay to delete this, Lawrence? LD: No, essential to story.] I am delighted he asked me to contribute to his book and hope it raises much-needed funds for the children's charity Wooden Spoon.

The 1991 World Cup is in the dim and distant past and it's easy to assume it must be difficult to remember much about a tournament way back then, but to be perfectly honest you never forget moments like winning a world championship and participating in the biggest tournament your sport has to offer. I was a relatively new member of the squad and took my lead from the more experienced players. Having said that, even I knew it was probably advisable to dilute severely anything David Campese said in private and completely ignore everything he said in public. He was a maverick who played over a hundred times for Australia, scoring sixty-four international tries, and enjoyed many moments of pure brilliance and the occasional flash of complete madness, but overall he was a player I would rather have in my team than on the other side. He had a reputation of winding up the opposition in a similar vein to the English hooker Brian Moore. The press enjoyed interviewing 'Campo' because he would always provide a quote or two, sometimes unintentionally.

On their way to the final England had played a successful forward-dominated game, the ball rarely making it past Rob Andrew at fly-half, who would invariably hoist a high kick in order to get his forwards on the front foot, thus keeping the opposition in defensive mode. Campo had a conversation with a few well-chosen journalists and told them England didn't have a chance in the final if they continued in that fashion. The only way to win, according to the expert Campo, would be to utilise the skill of Jeremy Guscott in the centre and the pace of winger Rory Underwood, in addition to the attacking threat of Jonathan Webb at full-back. The following day the papers were full of Campo's ramblings, which became a talking point amongst England supporters and presumably also the England team. I base this assumption on the fact they came at us right from the first whistle. Will Carling was making half breaks and feeding the ball to Guscott who was cutting us to ribbons. The ball made it to the wing on several occasions (several more times than in all their previous matches in the tournament combined) and it was only last-ditch Aussie tackling which prevented them from scoring. After about half an hour I remember my centre partner, Jason Little, looking at me gasping, 'Why can't Campo keep his f****** mouth shut. They're killing us.' Fortunately for some unknown reason England came out in the second half and reverted to the forward game which suited us much better.

The final whistle blew and we ran out 12–6 winners, an unforgettable moment for me and all my team-mates. Before the redevelopment, the showers and baths at Twickenham were adjacent to the changing rooms and the tubs themselves were large, individual ones standing on claw feet. I have fond memories of the Webb Ellis Cup being handed from bath to bath full of XXXX beer with players toasting the success and getting ready for a night of celebration. Eight years on and not a whole lot had changed. Sure, this time it was Cardiff not London, at the Millennium Stadium, and it was in spa baths that we were celebrating, but the trophy ('Bill' as the Aussies christened it) was still full of XXXX and being raucously passed from player to player.

Back to 1991. We left Twickenham on a fifty-two-seat coach that had at least 140 people on board including mums, dads, siblings, cousins, friends and a few random supporters who had somehow managed to gain access. Once again Bill was passed all around, constantly being refilled with any alcoholic drinks that came to hand. I recall looking at the scene, realising how much joy our achievement had brought to everyone on board and presumably Australians all over the world. It also occurred to me how devastated the England team and their supporters must have been. In that one moment the absolute definition of sport became clear: the ecstasy of winning and the abject agony of losing. Fortunately all of us on the bus were experiencing the former.

In 2003 I would have preferred an Australian victory, of course, but part of me (a very small part) was pleased the England team and the English nation could appreciate the unbridled joy of success in a World Cup. But hopefully it won't happen again for some time!

Whatever happens on the pitch in a game of rugby tends to stay on the pitch. By this I mean if there's been an indiscretion by player A against player B and player B doesn't have the time to exact suitable retribution before the final whistle, he will not try and sort it out off the pitch. He simply stores the incident away in an area of his brain that will be unlocked the next time the two players face each other on the field of play.

During my involvement in the sport at club and international level most players from opposing teams enjoyed each other's company after matches, either in the bar or at an official dinner. For people who have never played rugby it's probably difficult to believe that guys who spend eighty minutes knocking the hell out of each other then spend several hours having a few drinks, laughing and joking together. The only indicator of potential malice would be extremely subtle and usually delivered as the teams go their separate ways. A simple comment like 'See you in February' will be made from one player to another – and both would know what was really meant. A rough translation for the uninitiated would be, 'See you in February when we play again and I kick the crap out you.' The recipient of the comment would normally reply with a friendly smile saying, 'I'm looking forward to it already.'

My sense is that since the onset of professionalism teams spend less and less time with each other after matches, which in my humble opinion is a shame and detrimental to the game. It's now eight years since I retired but I still meet guys on a fairly regular basis from my time in the game and whoever it may be we have a common bond. In addition to the fact we played rugby against each other we also have shared off-pitch experiences. However, things change and I'm just glad I played in my era when mixing with the opposition was commonplace.

Will Carling was someone I had a good relationship with. We played against each other many times and enjoyed a number of beers together away from the game. I remember during the

1995 World Cup we shared training facilities with England at Newlands, Cape Town. They had the morning time slot and we took over for the afternoon. The England guys had finished and showered as we arrived, and Jason Little and I stopped to have a chat with Will and Jerry Guscott. We were having a laugh about various incidents which had occurred during the tournament and winding each other up about the imminent quarter-final between the two teams. After a few minutes a ringing sound emanated from Will's pocket. I remember being very impressed: mobile phones were still in their infancy in the mid-nineties. I know I didn't have one at the time, and if I had I wouldn't have had it in South Africa, where calls from Australia would have cost me a fortune. Will looked at the screen on his phone and clearly recognised the number. 'Excuse me guys, this is an important phone call, I'll have to take it,' he said as he walked away.

Jerry was left with us and in his own special way, raised an eyebrow and said, 'That'll be Diana. Again . . . ' I have no idea if the call was from the princess or not, but Jerry assured us it had been quite a regular occurrence during the tournament. In fact to make us feel better he said Will had left a team meeting the day before to take a call, so he was just as happy to 'sack' his own team-mates as he was a couple of Aussie centres. Unfortunately a couple of days later Will Carling, with his team this time, brushed us off once again in the quarter-final when Rob Andrew dropped a huge goal to secure victory for England.

Winning a World Cup is obviously the ultimate achievement in any sport and I was fortunate to experience it twice. Both moments will remain with me for ever. However, just as important as those times are the friends I made during my career in rugby, and I like to think I have many around the world, including the likes of Will, Jerry and in particular Lawrence.

All the best with the book, Lol.

Be Prepared

Rory Underwood

‘A few statistics on Rory. He won eighty-five England and six British and Irish Lions caps between 1984 and 1996, which at the time was an English record before it was surpassed by Jason Leonard and remains the highest total for an English back (at the time of writing Jonny Wilkinson is also on eighty-five caps for England). One record which does not look like falling in the near future is the forty-nine tries he scored whilst on international duty and it is interesting to note that in the matches in which Rory scored, England only lost five times. He is also a member of a small group of players to have represented their country at three World Cups.

‘I would describe Rory as the quiet man of the

team. Whilst team-mates would be tearing it up during post-match celebrations, as a non-drinker of alcohol Rory was always on hand to record events and was often sought out following a typical night of excess as a source of explanation for some otherwise inexplicable occurrence. There were wingers of his era who were quicker than Rory but no one had his knack of being in the right place at the right time, nor his ability to finish off a try with little space to work with. A true gent and one of life's good guys.'

Preparation is vital to everything you do in life. If you prepare well generally things go as you hope they will; conversely I'm sure many will recognise being in situations where a complete lack of preparation has had disastrous consequences. It might be a cliché, but only because it's true: 'If you fail to prepare, then you prepare to fail.'

Looking back at the World Cup of 1991, at the time I felt we prepared well but with hindsight perhaps not as thoroughly as we could have. In fact if I compare our feeble efforts on the preparation front to the 2003 World Cup campaign led by Clive Woodward, it appears we left most things to luck and chance.

In order to get an idea of how the All Blacks played their rugby, the England management decided to show us a video of an England–New Zealand fixture at Twickenham, the venue for our opening match against them in 1991. In order to bolster the confidence of the squad they decided the match should also show England winning. Fair enough. Good strategy.

Unfortunately they had to search back eight years into the archives, to November 1983, to find what they were looking for. And thank God England did pull off that victory, because prior to that the last win at Twickenham came in January 1936 courtesy of two tries from Prince Alexander Obolensky! (It has taken another seventy-five years for there to be another royal connection on the field of English rugby. Congratulations Mike.) Anyway, we all watched the match and spent most of the time taking the piss (from a safe distance) out of Peter Winterbottom, who was the only player in the current squad playing in the fixture. Lots of comments were made about hairstyles and tight shorts and I was as vocal as anyone, until it dawned on me I made my own international debut three months after the match took place.

Mentioning tight shorts reminds me of a particular kit issue we had prior to the opening match. For several years Gymflex had been our suppliers and everyone in the team had become used to the style and fit, but just before the 1991 World Cup the Rugby Football Union agreed a contract with Cotton Traders to supply England. You may or may not be aware former England prop forward and captain Fran Cotton is the Managing Director of Cotton Traders, and his patriotic involvement perhaps goes some way towards explaining the design feature of the shorts.

Traditionally, the match-day kit is hung in the changing rooms prior to the arrival of the players, but to make it more of an occasion it was decided to present the players with their kit two days before the match in a small ceremony. As the team was announced, each player walked forward and received his kit from our coach Geoff Cooke whilst all the other players applauded. We were then told to go and try it on to check there were no problems. To be honest most of the shirts were fine, although one of the sleeves on mine was slightly longer than the other (only joking, Fran, all three sleeves were exactly the same length). When it came to the shorts, however, we had a problem. In order to get the crutch of the shorts in the right place the waistband had to be located somewhere between your chest and your chin. Conversely, if the waistband was in the correct position the crutch hung down like a sodden nappy just below knee level. You'll appreciate this had no effect on the front five, but the back-row boys and the backs were not going to be seen in private, let alone in front of 70,000 at Twickenham, and a global TV audience of millions, wearing these ridiculous garments.

Under normal circumstances this would not have been a major problem. Previously England shorts had been all white and readily available at all good retailers. But these were not 'normal circumstances'. This time our shorts had been 'designed'. Cotton Traders had decided to spice things up a bit by embroidering the rose of England on the right leg of each pair (nice) and a jazzy blue square motif on the left (inexplicable). Our team manager was despatched to Twickenham to collect a variety of different-sized old-style white shorts from the 'kit cupboard'. They were distributed and everyone was happy, everyone that is except Cotton Traders.

They had signed an exclusive deal with the RFU to supply the kit and presumably paid a decent sum of money for the privilege. So at the very least they would be looking for some serious financial compensation if the shorts were not worn. They had also taken the promotional photography of the 'New England Kit' and had a warehouse full of stock ready for distribution after everyone saw the opening game and would be scrambling to get their hands on the new designer England gear. So with less than forty-eight hours to go before kick-off, the England management were scouring Yellow Pages in search of a seamstress (or several) who could cut out the rose and the blue square and sew them onto pristine white shorts. As I said, preparation is king.

Something else we had to prepare for was the haka. We actually had a team meeting to discuss what we should do when the All Blacks threw down their famous challenge. Perhaps we should just ignore it and continue to warm up? Maybe we should fight fire with fire and do a Morris dance? It seemed as though we were in a no-win situation and as the discussion continued it was agreed that if we ignored them it would piss them off and probably make them play better, and if we faced up to them and accepted the challenge that would also fire them up to perform. We eventually narrowed our options down to two possibilities. The backs were keen to ignore the haka whilst the forwards wanted to fight. As with all good democracies we compromised: it was decided to get into a circular huddle allowing the three-quarters to have their backs to the 'dance' and the forwards could eyeball the opposition and let the adrenalin flow. In addition, we were going to keep our tracksuits on for the performance, which meant that when it was finished we could casually stroll over to the touchline and take an inordinate amount of time stripping down to our kit. This would create more time for the All Blacks to come down from the fever pitch we knew they would have reached by the end of the haka. All round, not a bad plan.

On the day of the match the All Blacks made their way to their starting positions, we gathered in a circle. As the haka started, so did the crowd. As Lawrence mentioned at the beginning, I played eighty-five times for England over a twelve-year span. Throughout that period I never heard a noise like that one. The crowd were cheering, singing, and roaring (I think they must have thought we were in with a chance). As a result we didn't hear one word of the haka, in fact we were still in our circle long after they'd finished. When we broke up we noticed every All Black in his starting position ready for the match to begin. Meanwhile we had a referee telling us we had less than thirty seconds before he blew his whistle to start the game (something to do with the TV schedule).

Tracksuits are not particularly easy to slip on or off at the best of times, and when you're under pressure you can guarantee a boot gets caught inside a tracksuit bottom and a zip gets stuck on the jacket. We looked ridiculous as we tried desperately to separate ourselves from the extra apparel. Players were hopping around and falling over in their attempts to remove the tracksuits. Consequently, as the referee blew his whistle the All Blacks were perfectly prepared and composed whilst some of the England team had not even reached their starting positions.

Looking back, we took part in a lot of team meetings to discuss various issues. In reality we should have spent more time on the training pitch preparing ourselves physically and mentally for the challenge of a World Cup and an opening game against the reigning world champions. On 3 October 1991 we were lucky to only lose by 12–18. That said, we did go on to contest the final a month later and the All Blacks lost in their semi-final against Australia, so we must have done something right. Perhaps it was the shorts.

1995

The third World Cup was for many more emotional than either of the first two, not least because it officially proclaimed the return of hosts South Africa to the world rugby stage. Australia were favourites to win after twelve months of unbeaten Test rugby; however, the Springboks proved they hadn't lost their touch during the years of isolation as they beat the defending champions 27–18 in the opening match.

Pool matches saw some incredible performances, notably the 24–23 victory by Ireland over Wales which once again saw that proud rugby nation leave the tournament before the knockout stages. The tournament also revealed a twenty-year-old who literally burst onto the scene and become the icon of the World Cup, New Zealand's massive left-wing Jonah Lomu. He certainly left his mark on international rugby (in addition to leaving his mark on several players) and scored tries practically at will. Almost overnight this 6ft 5in, 19st battering ram, who could run the 100 metres in about eleven seconds, became a phenomenon. He was scary enough performing the haka; at full pelt he became truly frightening.

England played Australia in the quarter-final and Rob Andrew's dropped goal in the final minute of extra-time knocked the favourites out. It was a tough defeat for the Australians to take, having harboured such high hopes of retaining the Webb Ellis Cup when the tournament began. The English supporters, however, revelled in the victory, as John Eales, one of the Australian locks playing that day, recalls.

'Walking off the pitch I felt the disappointment of defeat, and in the days that followed the feeling grew rather than subsided. We had a World Cup song which had been sung ad nauseam throughout the campaign and one of the lines was "We've won the cup, we ain't giving it up." When we arrived back at the team hotel we were greeted by rugby's equivalent of cricket's Barmy Army. Hundreds of English rugby supporters, all singing our song with a few word changes: "You've lost the cup, you stuffed it up." I think it was "stuffed" anyway.'

Poor lambs. And if that wasn't bad enough, worse was to follow for John and his team-mates. Following their exit from the tournament they headed straight home and it was while they were in transit at Perth airport that perhaps the full impact of the defeat hit them. Rugby is all about the supporters and as a player, knowing you have let down those that follow you and cheer you on is worse than your personal disappointment. In 1995 Australia were confronted by this reality almost face to face.

'We were in Perth airport at the same time a planeload of Australians were going the other way, heading to South Africa to watch us play in the semi-final of the World Cup! It was an awful moment. Their expectations had obviously been as high as ours, and as a result they had booked the trip many weeks or months in advance. We had let them down, and now they were on their way to watch England against New Zealand, a match they wouldn't normally cross the road to glance at if they hadn't already paid thousands of dollars for the trip. This was an exceptionally 'ordinary' moment for me, probably the lowest in my entire rugby career.'

The England team were to face their own low moment not long after John's airport encounter when Jonah Lomu almost single-handedly tore them apart in the semi-final but I'll leave it to others in the stories that follow to relive the big man's astonishing impact. In the other semi-final in Durban South Africa beat France in a match played from start to finish in a rain storm so heavy that there were moments just before, and even during, the game when abandonment seemed the only option. Interestingly, if the game had not been played, France would have gone through due to a better disciplinary record. What that would have done to the history of the game, one can only guess at.

The final was played at Ellis Park in Johannesburg between New Zealand and South Africa and after eighty minutes the scores stood at 9–9. The match went into extra-time and it came down to the Springboks' fly-half Joel Stransky to kick the winning dropped goal for a 15–12 South African victory.

There is no doubt that the most memorable moment of the tournament was Nelson Mandela, recently released after twenty-seven years in prison on Robben Island and wearing a replica of the Springbok captain François Pienaar's jersey with a number 6 on the back, presenting the trophy in Johannesburg on Saturday 24 June to François and thanking the South African team for what they had done for the country. 'One team, one country,' he cried. From that moment a party started in South Africa that some say lasted for four days.

A couple of weeks after the final reports began to circulate that were to have a massive impact on the game of rugby. It was being said that hundreds of the world's best players had signed up for a super league after being offered large financial inducements. The amateur game was cracking at the seams and it was just weeks after these rumours broke that the game of rugby union entered the professional era on 26 August 1995. Thoughts ten years earlier that a World Cup competition would help prevent the game becoming professional had, if anything, accelerated it towards professionalism.

What Did Suzie Do Next?

Having been a member of England's victorious World Cup sevens team in 1993 and gaining selection to tour South Africa a year later, I felt I stood a chance of making the squad in 1995. But on the day of the announcement, no matter how many times I listened to the radio or read the press my name was nowhere to be seen or heard. As an ambitious player I wanted to be involved and was hugely disappointed when the Bath No. 8 Steve Ojomo received the nod ahead of me. However, looking on the bright side I did not run across, or probably more accurately get run over by, Jonah Lomu. Every cloud and all that.

I'm not certain of the validity of this story but I have heard it told on several occasions. Apparently James Small, the South African winger in 1995, was a little bit concerned about facing Jonah in the World Cup final and requested a meeting with the team coach Kitch Christie. James asked Kitch for advice on how to defend against the giant All Black and in a very relaxed manner, Kitch explained how simple it was. 'All you have to do when he's running towards you is to get on his outside and shepherd him infield. This will give our back row and centres the chance to climb all over him and bring him down.'

'But what if Jonah makes an outside break?' asked James.

'I've thought of that as well,' replied Kitch. 'You need to stay on his inside and force him towards the touchline, which will become our sixteenth player, keeping him on the field of play. As he straightens up, once again our back row and centres should be across in time to bring him down.'

Thinking he had covered all the bases, Kitch stood to leave the room when James piped up again. 'What if he runs straight at me?'

'Ah, now this scenario is simple. All you need to do is turn around, bend down, pick up a piece of shit and throw it at him. With a bit of luck he'll be distracted and forced to slow down.'

James thought about this unusual piece of advice and asked the obvious question. 'What if there isn't a piece of shit behind me?'

'Believe me, if he's running straight at you, there will be,' was the reply. And apparently there was!

Incidentally, Kitch Christie was the South African coach from 1994 to 1996 and was unbeaten during this period, leading his country to a then record fourteen consecutive victories, one of which was the 1995 World Cup final, the first tournament they had been allowed to participate in in the post-apartheid era. Not a bad record.

Whilst I wasn't involved in 1995, I was close to the squad and have heard numerous tales from the boys who played, one of which involves the third- and fourth-place playoff match. If there is a more inconsequential game in rugby, I don't know it. Who cares who comes third? Whichever countries are participating, one assumes they gave their all throughout the tournament and came up short at the semi-final stage. To then make them play a further match seems ludicrous to me, and also to the England team of 1995 apparently.

The players were not interested in the fixture and the majority of them decided to go to a bar the night before the game for a couple of quiet beers and reflect on the tournament before returning home a few days later. As they walked in they could hear a loud party taking place at the back of the bar, champagne flowing and the distinctive smell of Gauloises cigarettes. Closer inspection revealed it was the French team, England's opponents the following day. Clearly they had a similar opinion on the importance of a playoff. Although France had started their party before England and continued after the English left, they still ran out 19–9 winners in the 'crucial' match a few hours later. French flair or a relaxed approach? I'll leave it with you. Mind you, England may have been a little premature in dismissing the match. It was subsequently discovered that the team securing third in 1995 gained automatic qualification to the 1999 tournament, while the team finishing fourth had to qualify (oops).

The final between New Zealand and South Africa was another match that could not be decided in eighty minutes, and once again it took a dropped goal to secure South Africa's 15–12 victory. It was something of a miracle the All Blacks lasted through extra-time as the majority of the side had succumbed to severe food poisoning forty-eight hours earlier, and ever since the match there has been a series of conspiracy theories. Had the chilli sauce, chicken burgers or sweet and sour prawns served to the team been poisoned by a waitress known as 'Suzie'? Nothing was ever proved but the incident does highlight how players' diets have changed with the advent of professionalism. I can't imagine chicken burgers or sweet and sour prawns being on the modern player's menu, at least not during a World Cup tournament. Just goes to show, not everything about the modern game is an improvement.

Tight as Newts

François Pienaar

'François is arguably most famous for being captain of the first Springbok team to lift the World Cup. Before the 1995 tournament the Springboks were seeded only ninth and were certainly not expected to dethrone the incumbent champions Australia.

'All rugby followers will remember the remarkable post-match presentation ceremony with Nelson Mandela, but may have forgotten François's acceptance speech, where he made it clear the team had won the trophy not just for the 60,000 fans at Ellis Park, but also for all 43,000,000 South Africans. It was the dawn of the Rainbow Nation.

'I got to know François well when he moved to the UK in 1997 and became player-coach at

Saracens. In fact I'm not sure I've forgiven him and his team for inflicting defeat on Wasps in the 1998 Pilkington Cup final.

'As a player he was uncompromising, and when you look at the record of Saracens during his tenure you realise he was some coach as well. I think they qualified for the Heineken Cup during each of his four years' involvement. François writes as captain of a World Cup-winning team and previous winner of the prestigious International Player of the Year award, and I am delighted he has made a contribution to this book.'

Friday 1 April 2011

I received a phone call this morning from Lawrence Dallaglio asking me if I would contribute a World Cup memory for a book he was producing. As a fellow rugby player and friend I was more than happy to help.

'What sort of thing are you looking for?'

'To be honest any recollection at all that you have of the 1995 tournament and preferably something humorous.'

'If you want something humorous, why are you ringing me?' I enquired. 'I don't do humour, you know that.'

'Well, perhaps something informative then.'

As I was speaking I looked up at a calendar hanging from the wall in my office and I knew he was winding me up. The conversation carried on for several more minutes in which he explained about Wooden Spoon, the benefiting charity, and shared with me a couple of stories which had already been submitted. We said our goodbyes and I put the phone down. I was being set up for something, but I didn't know what. Anyway I had an hour to spare and decided to scribble something down, but I want everyone to know I wasn't taken in by his April Fool's phone call. I'm not certain how the following is going to come back and bite me in the arse, but the one thing I am absolutely certain of is that it will not appear in Lol's mythical World Cup book. So with that in mind, here goes.

As I said, I don't do humour. Nevertheless, I would like to share with you a decision I made as captain in 1995 which I genuinely feel was instrumental in helping us win the opening match of the World Cup and set the tone for the rest of the campaign. Hopefully it will illustrate that a captain's role does not start with the first whistle of a match and end with the last. There are so many things you need to consider, from team dynamics through to selection, strategy and game plans.

Our opening encounter was against Australia, favourites and undefeated in the twelve months leading up to the tournament. We knew if we beat them we would have a potentially easier route to negotiate through to the final. There are no easy ways to win a World Cup, but topping your pool helps as it allows you to play a team in the quarter-final who finished second in their group. All our preparation had been geared towards beating this Australian side, which featured a fantastic pack of forwards including Phil Kearns, John Eales and 'Willie' Ofahengaue to name just three.

Most rugby matches, in particular Test matches, are won and lost up front. There's an old saying in rugby, 'Forwards win matches, backs just decide by how many.' As a back-row forward I couldn't agree more. We needed not only to take them on and match them up front, but to dominate them. No mean feat. We had several weeks' training before the tournament and things were going okay, not great but okay. Something was missing, particularly amongst the tight five (front row and second row). With less than a week to go to the match I made a decision which a modern-day management team would probably not allow.

I arranged for two limousines to arrive at our hotel and take every squad member in the tight five out for the evening. This amounted to about ten or eleven players. Now, limousines in South Africa in the mid-nineties were hardly commonplace. In fact it proved extremely difficult to locate any as it soon became apparent pretty much all we had were ox wagons and normal cars. However, after countless phone calls I found what I was looking for and they both arrived at the appointed hour. I had earlier briefed the guys selected for the trip. I told them the limousines were at their disposal and what they did with them was of no concern to me or the management. In addition I spoke to our coach and we cancelled training the following day. All I asked of them was to return whenever they wanted with a plan to beat Australia.

To this day I have no idea where they went or what they did. They arrived back at the team hotel in the small hours and we met at 10.00 a.m. in the team room. Looking into their eyes it was obvious they had not spent the night in Annie's Tea Room or indeed the local spa. We talked for no longer than five minutes, and as the room quickly filled with the stale fumes of a good night out, it was clear to me they had formed a 'brotherhood'.

What you need to understand is that prior to 1995, during the apartheid regime, our 'Test match' arena was to play against each other (South Africa having been banned from the world of international rugby). So when Northern Transvaal guys played against Western Province, for instance, it was nothing short of warfare. There was no love lost whatsoever. This had been the case for more than a generation. As there was no national team to play for, we had little or no understanding of how to forge together as a unit. All we knew was how to beat each other up. So although we were about to represent South Africa in the World Cup, there was a degree of distrust, to a greater or lesser extent, between the players from the various provinces.

Through the fumes l could see a group of guys who were quite jovial, yet a little jaded, definitely focussed and most important of all, they sat there as friends. At the very next training session and for the rest of the tournament their contribution was immense. I've already used the word, but they had genuinely formed a brotherhood. It was as if there was nothing they wouldn't do for each other and I like to think the decision to find the transport and give them a free hand for a few hours contributed to their transformation.

To exemplify this bond I recall our semi-final match in the driving rain against France in Durban. We had built a decent lead during the first fifty or so minutes and then froze slightly, attempting to protect our position. This allowed France to play some of the rugby they are renowned for and before long there were no more than a handful of points between the sides. I will always remember the giant French No. 8 Abdelatif Benazzi almost scoring in the closing minutes. To be honest I thought he had succeeded but the referee, Derek Bevan, made the right decision as subsequent replays showed Benazzi's arm separated the ball from the try line. At the ensuing five-metre scrum we were under huge pressure as the French put about a dozen players into their pack to try and secure a pushover try. The scrum broke up and just before it reformed I saw Kobus Wiese grab his second-row partner and say, 'In this scrum you can go up, you can go down, but you are *not* going back.' The scrum held firm and we made the final primarily due to the tight five who didn't give an inch.

Finally, I'm often asked if I had any official role during the filming of the 2009 movie *Invictus*, the story of how Nelson Mandela joined forces with the South African rugby team in 1995 to help unite the country. The answer is no, I was not involved in an advisory capacity although I did get to meet several of the stars including Morgan Freeman (playing Nelson Mandela) and Matt Damon (playing me). I had a couple of very good nights with Matt, who at 5ft 10in and around 12st (75kg) was always going to find it difficult to play me at 6ft 3in and 17st (110kg), but as an award-winning actor he was used to overcoming such minor problems. Yet another factor which did not work in his favour was the simple fact he's an extremely handsome man. The make-up department were going to have a major job making his face look like it had been set on fire and put out with a razor blade, which mine clearly now resembles after all the stitches I collected during a career in rugby.

During one night out whilst drinking red wine I mentioned to him that a couple of friends and I were going to climb Kilimanjaro and then compete in the Cape Argus Pick n Pay Tour, which is one of the largest sporting events in the world with in excess of 35,000 competitors racing around the Cape peninsula over a 110km course. Matt said he would love to join us on the climb but once we explained the timeframe it became clear that it would be impossible given his schedule commitments, but he said he would compete in the race (by this stage we'd had a glass or three). He phoned his brother in America who is a keen triathlete and asked him if he fancied taking part on a tandem. Within a couple of days his brother arrived and the two of them, together with me and a friend of mine, took part in the race aboard a couple of bicycles made for two. It's testament to the spirit of Matt Damon that he undertook the challenge, especially when you consider he was not a cyclist, the weather conditions were the worst in living memory with severe gale-force winds, and all his people kept urging him not to compete, obviously fearing he might be blown off his bike and scarred (which I suppose might have helped his physical portrayal of me hugely). Anyway, we all finished the race unscathed. So it was as a result of the film that I had my brief encounter with American film royalty. It was fun to have a brief glimpse through that window, to witness the lives of global celebrities, but nothing will ever come close to the feeling I had in 1995 when Nelson Mandela presented me with the Webb Ellis Cup.

Lawrence, I may have just wasted an hour of my life writing this, and if it proves to be the case I *will* catch up with you one day, my friend. But if your request was genuine I wish you every success with the book.

Touch and Go

Jerry Guscott

‘Described as a precocious talent, amongst other things, Jerry made some impact on his England debut in 1989 when he introduced himself onto the international scene with a hat-trick of tries. One of the best of his generation, possibly any generation, he seemed to have it all in terms of skill, which when added to his exceptional pace and vision produced a formidable player. Less than a month after his debut he gained selection for the Lions tour to Australia, where he produced a decisive "Boy's Own" try in the second Test, collecting his own grubber kick to score next to the posts. In the third Test Australian "superstar" David Campese made a serious blunder behind his own line, allowing Ieuan Evans to score the simplest of tries and clinch the

series. (Really there is no reason for mentioning this in a Jerry Guscott introduction other than to let you know how much I enjoy reminding myself of this mishap by the "great man" at any opportunity.) Eight years later he added to his extensive list of magical moments when scoring the winning dropped goal in the decisive second Test match.

'Very few players can put three World Cup campaigns, three British and Irish Lions tours and thirty tries for England on their sporting CV. Jerry achieved this feat and thankfully is now of an age when he no longer feels it necessary to remind me how good he used to be when we meet up from time to time!'

The 1995 Rugby World Cup was a tremendous advertisement for the game. It was an exciting tournament, often very entertaining. The fact that South Africa is in the European time zone meant it was broadcast during peak hours on network television throughout the continent, ensuring huge viewing figures. The sad aspect, however, was that very little of the entertaining and exciting rugby was played by England. Many will remember our quarter-final against Australia when Rob Andrew dropped a goal in the dying seconds to secure victory, but even this was not a classic game, just a good contest.

Having arrived in Durban, one of the things everyone was

looking forward to (not) was the welcome lunch in Cape Town; every participating team had been summoned no matter where they were based. Just what we needed after a long flight was a 6.15 a.m. alarm call, a quick breakfast and a trip to a tiny airport where we shared the waiting room with the Argentine team (our first opposition) until our delayed flight took off. When we eventually got airborne, the plane proceeded to hop around the country picking up other teams. Perfect. At the function, held in a giant tent at the Groot Constantia Wine estate were 416 players, plus their respective management, all in a competition to see who could look the most pissed off.

The Australians were deemed to be the winners – in addition to the obvious reasons for being thoroughly unamused, they were kitted out in green and yellow blazers which would have looked perfect at Henley Regatta. I am sure you can imagine the stick they received from most of the other teams. The Ivory Coast squad were the only guys who looked genuinely happy to be there. They spent most of the time collecting autographs and posing for photographs with the better known players, illustrating how pleased they were just to make the final stages.

When the tournament finally started, we fulfilled to the letter Jack Rowell's final pronouncement that England 'must hit the ground running'. We were true to his words; unfortunately the direction in which we ran was backwards. We had trouble in the scrums, did not play at all well and were lucky to win the match 24–18. In fact, if Argentina had had a goal kicker that day, we would have lost. This was still the amateur era (just) and not all our preparation was as good as it could have been. To combat the heat and humidity we had been given salt tablets on a regular basis, but after two weeks we were told they combined badly with the isotonic drink we were also taking, causing some kind of reaction which made everyone feel lethargic. I dread to think what the result against New Zealand would have been if we were still taking the combination at the semi-final stage (they would have needed a cricket scoreboard).

On the eve of the quarter final against the boys with the green and yellow blazers, Austin Swain, our psychologist, gave us a mental exercise to complete. He produced a sheet of paper with the numbers 1 to 21 printed down the side representing the team and replacements. He asked us to write something positive about each name on the list. We then had to cut up the paper and put each comment in the relevant envelope. Later that evening he slipped the envelopes under the door of each player's room. All comments were anonymous so I'm not sure who wrote, 'You look very clean and tidy in your England kit' as their comment for me. Equally, Martin Bayfield (our 6ft 10in second row) never found out who wrote 'You are very tall' as one of his affirmations, but Mike Catt or possibly Jason Leonard would get my vote. Joking aside, this was a genuinely useful exercise with the vast majority of comments very positive. It made a real difference knowing those thoughts were circulating among the guys you were playing with.

I will cover the quarter-final and semi-final very quickly, we won one in the last minute and to all intents and purposes lost the other in the first minute. I'm sure others will cover both games more than adequately.

I took my rugby seriously and disliked losing intensely, but I was not one to mope around after a defeat. You can look as sad and desolate as you like but it's not going to change the result. Following the semi-final I joined all the other players in the dressing room holding my head in my hands, staring at the floor. From time to time I had a little peep to see if everyone was maintaining the same grieving posture. Almost to a man they were, with the exception of Jason Leonard, who caught my eye, winked, and raised his hand to his mouth indicating he was ready for a beer. Like me, Jason despised losing but knew shedding a few tears was not going to make any difference.

Following the defeat we had to return to Johannesburg and shared the same flight as the All Blacks. As we boarded the plane they had already taken their seats in business class as we turned right and made our way to economy. I remember talking to Eric Rush, the New Zealand winger, who said there was a huge amount of surreptitious piss-taking and hand signals as we took our seats. To be fair we would have done the same if the roles had been reversed.

Back in Johannesburg we prepared for the third- and fourth-place playoff match. I say 'prepared' but that is probably not a great description. We filled in time between the loss to New Zealand and our match against the French by playing a bit of touch rugby. Mind you, even that can get a little heated from time to time. Usually it starts off fine, until someone 'touches' someone else a little roughly and before you know it, it's full-on contact. I remember one particular session during which things were most certainly heading in this direction; the session was potentially one incident away from getting completely out of hand. The ball was passed to our back-row forward Tim Rodber, not the best delivery I've ever seen because even though Tim is 6ft 6in tall even he had to leap vertically to gather it. I was on the opposition, directly opposite Tim, and saw this as an opportunity. With Tim at full stretch, I arrived at full tilt and drilled my shoulder into his rib cage, wrapping my arms around him as my momentum drove him back. At precisely that moment a scream of pain reminded me of something – Tim had quite seriously injured his ribs in the semi-final (oops). What flashed through my mind next was that I was potentially seconds away from a severe beating.

My only option was to hold on to Tim as tightly as I could, thereby reducing the distance from which he could land a punch on me. Less momentum, I reasoned, equalled less pain. If I could hold on for a few seconds a rescue party would surely arrive to save me. Fortunately this is exactly what happened. Tim managed a couple of ineffective blows on the top of my head as I hung on for dear life before a few of the lads piled in and broke up what would have been a very one-sided encounter.

I should have left it at that but couldn't resist a parting shot at Tim (from a safe distance). 'You were bloody lucky the boys turned up and saved you. Another few seconds and I'd have kicked your ass.'

Fee, Fie, Foe Fum, I Smell the Blood . . .

Phil de Glanville

'Phil was a centre who played in thirty-eight internationals for England, a remarkable achievement when you consider he was on the scene at the same time as Will Carling (captain) and Jerry Guscott (one of the world's best), neither of whom seemed to sustain any injuries or noticeable loss of form. When he first arrived in the England squad he was widely known as "Hollywood", largely due to his film star looks. Thinking back now, I am beginning to suspect Phil came up with the name himself. Whoever did, I'm pleased to say after just a few seasons of rugby at club and international level the sobriquet became nothing more than a distant memory. In fairness

this was always going to be the case as he was an uncompromising, tough player completely committed in attack and defence.

'After Carling stepped down as captain, the honour was passed on to Phil, not necessarily everyone's choice for the role but he conducted himself well and won many of his critics over during his spell in charge. He eventually lost his place to a certain Will Greenwood, who became a mainstay in the side for several years to come. Our international careers overlapped for a couple of seasons during which time I witnessed Phil's ability from close range and became a big fan of his determination and tenacity.'

One memory that has remained with me ever since our semi-final at Newlands, Cape Town, against New Zealand in the 1995 World Cup concerns the All Black phenomenon Jonah Lomu. Several other English players have lifelong memories from that game, but for different reasons.

During this period of my international career I was frequently selected to sit on the English bench and the semi-final was no different. Whilst it's still an honour, and there's always the chance you'll make an appearance during the game, it's also very frustrating because deep down you feel as though you're good enough to play from the start. I played in the centre, as Lawrence has kindly pointed out, the same positions as Carling and Guscott, so it was always going to be difficult to break that particular partnership. However, it didn't stop me having a heated discussion with our team manager, Jack Rowell, about my inclusion, or rather lack of. Jack had been my club coach for several years at Bath and had therefore seen me play often enough to know exactly what I was capable of. Unfortunately, as Jerry Guscott was a team-mate at Bath he'd also seen just as much of him and knew about all his obvious talents. As usual, Jack listened intently to what I had to say, and then ignored it completely. I was on the bench, end of story.

After a quarter of this game, however, there was only one place I would rather have been than on the bench, and that was in the stand with the rest of the England support. We were being absolutely steamrollered by Lomu. He'd shown in previous rounds he was a threat and someone who would require close marking, but no one expected the one-man demolition he produced that day. The contest was as good as over after twenty-five minutes, as Lomu made a mockery of every Englishman who tried to get in his way. Most famously, he swatted away Tony Underwood, tore past Will Carling and bulldozed Mike Catt on his way to his first try. Jonah, at just twenty years of age, crossed the English line four times during the game, demonstrating his immense power and pace. It was a classic case of 'a man against boys'. The game became even more farcical when the New Zealand No. 8 Zinzan Brooke dropped a goal from nearly fifty metres out. In those days replacements were only allowed if there was an injury on the field of play – it would be a couple more seasons before tactical substitutions were sanctioned (thank God). For forty minutes, as I sat and watched the most one-sided match imaginable, I prayed there would be no injuries.

At half-time, there was little Jack could say to the team other than talk about personal pride. Every player needed to 'stand up and be counted'. There was no place to hide.

During the second half the England performance improved, which I accept may have had something to do with New Zealand taking their foot off the pedal as victory had been all but assured. However, we scored a couple of tries which if nothing else made the scoreline a bit more respectable, and suddenly I wanted to get on to the pitch, although of course I certainly wasn't wishing for an injury to one of our players. That aside, I genuinely felt I could make a difference to our performance, briefly even convincing myself that I could do in the second half to New Zealand what Jonah had done to us in the first. I can only assume the sun had got to me by then. Only trouble was, I was so excited at the prospect of playing, coupled with over-hydrating while sitting on the bench, that I had an almost uncontrollable urge to go to the toilet. I spent several minutes squirming in my seat and 'holding on' but with just a few minutes of the match remaining I couldn't last any longer and I decided to rush back to the loo in the changing rooms.

When you leave the pitch at Newlands there are a series of steps leading down into the bowels of the stand where the changing rooms are situated. The steps are extremely narrow, not something you'd expect in such a big ground. In fact, there's barely enough room for two people to pass without some expert manoeuvring. I completed my business and ran back towards the pitch, still hopeful I might get on if only for a minute or two. I took the stairs three at a time and about halfway up everything went completely black. It was as if all the lights had been switched off. I looked ahead towards the top of the stairs and could make out the silhouette of Jonah Lomu virtually blocking out all the available light. He looked like a giant standing there, baying for English blood, and I realised instantly that the match must be over and the players leaving the pitch. Clearly Jonah was keen to be first back to the All Blacks changing room. And all that was standing in his way was me!

Assuming my end was nigh, I took a deep breath and continued up the stairs towards the massive frame looming ahead. Having taken a few steps himself, Jonah noticed me on my way up and incredibly backed out of the narrow tunnel allowing me to continue. I reached the top and shook his hand, congratulating him on his performance. He nodded his appreciation and disappeared into the tunnel and down the steps. The next person I saw was Jack Rowell, who had seen Jonah reversing out of the tunnel. 'Bloody hell, Phil,' Jack said. 'Not only have you managed to stop Lomu, but you forced him to take a backward step! And I didn't even select you. Sorry about that.'

I'd like to think he meant it, but in reality that was typical Jack Rowell humour.

'Mr Ambassador, with these Stories . . .'

Jason Leonard

'Jason is Lead Ambassador for the children's charity Wooden Spoon which is a beneficiary of this project, and has kindly supplied a couple of tales for this book (with which, as the title above suggests, he is "spoiling us"). He also features in several others.

'Anyone with a passing interest in the world of rugby will know the name Jason Leonard. For a period of time he was the world's most capped player (119 including British and Irish Lions) and is currently the world's most capped forward. He won four Grand Slams and a World Cup with England and was a member of the victorious Lions tour to South Africa in 1997, all of which doesn't begin to tell you anything about the man. He straddled the amateur and professional eras and always retained some of the important social values of this great sport. Beer has always been synonymous with rugby and Jason was never going to allow the link to be severed during his time in the game. He would always take new members of the team under his wing and share a few stories and drinks with them – in his words, "To make them feel as though they belonged." All very admirable, but on more than one occasion the newcomer would arrive back at the team hotel draped off the shoulder of the great man, completely incapacitated.

'He was my training partner for years and my room-mate on more occasions than I care to remember. To be fair we were perfectly suited as roomies, dovetailing well. Invariably he would be on his way out as I was coming in (well, perhaps not "invariably"). His rugby record is available for all to see; regarding the man, he always seems to find time to speak to everyone – and I mean everyone. Jason is one of life's good guys, prepared to lend a hand if he possibly can, particularly if he can be holding a drink in it at the same time.'

On Thin Ice

When Lawrence asked me to become involved in this World Cup memories book, I was delighted to help out. I took part in four World Cup campaigns and have several stories which I'd happily commit to print, together with a few which will definitely remain out of the public domain! If only he hadn't told me one of my favourite charities, Wooden Spoon, would be benefiting financially from the book. I was appointed as Lead Ambassador to the charity in January 2009 and according to their website my role is as follows:

'Jason acts as the Charity's key advocate, promoting the Charity's work at a national level to decision makers, organisations and the government.'

This makes me sound like a relatively serious individual, but in order to make my World Cup memories interesting I know I'm not going to portray myself in the best possible light. More worrying still is the thought of certain players around the world including me in their recollections. Even allowing for the legal department throwing out any dodgy contributions, I suspect Wooden Spoon may now seriously question their wisdom in appointing me to assist in promoting the charity at a national level. Oh well, it was fun while it lasted and I hope I did some good.

It's well known in rugby circles that I like the occasional drink and while I see little problem with that, the revelation coming later in this book from my England team-mate Josh Lewsey, concerning the lengths to which he was prepared to go in order to avoid a couple of in-flight sharpeners on the plane home from

Australia in 2003 after we'd won the World Cup, made me wonder if my reputation hadn't perhaps become a little exaggerated. I decided on some scientific research to unearth the truth. I googled 'Jason Leonard drinking' and was more than a little surprised to see the search engine found 3,800,000 results in 0.25 seconds. Such evidence may indicate Josh had at least some basis for his concerns, I suppose.

I was fortunate in the timing of my career as I spanned the amateur and professional eras; obviously post-1995 when money was finally introduced (legally) to the game the approach and attitude of players had to change. It was no longer sufficient merely to turn up and train a couple of times a week while looking to spend as many hours as possible in the pub with your mates. Change happened virtually overnight; it seemed as though every day was taken up with training, resting, studying rugby videos, talking about opposition teams, discussing tactics etc. Whilst I embraced the new world I was never going to abandon all my amateur roots, so I decided to train full-time with Harlequins and England and also see if I could continue to get away with a few visits to the boozer, just for a bit of relaxation you understand.

I remember on the eve of departure for the 1995 World Cup in South Africa, team manager Jack Rowell called a meeting of the squad to discuss an important issue. We all arrived in the team room at the Petersham Hotel in Richmond, took our seats and waited for the man to arrive. He walked in, very smart, on the stroke of 8.00 p.m. You don't become managing director of Golden Wonder by being late, or not wearing a crisp suit (sorry, couldn't resist it!).

Jack was seeking support for an idea he had, which he believed would give England an edge in achieving the dream of World Cup victory. He wanted the entire squad to adhere to a 'voluntary' booze ban for the duration of the tournament. He put his side very eloquently, pointing out it would be a small price to pay for the ultimate prize in rugby, and if we did win then we'd all participate in the biggest party the world had ever seen. It was difficult to argue against his clear rationale, although a few of us did give it a go. I suggested banning drinking sessions but allowing the occasional evening beer to help get some sleep, to which 'The Pitbull' Brian Moore shouted, 'When has just one beer been sufficient to put you to sleep?' After a healthy debate it was decided Jack was right and the squad were going to abstain from that moment on.

Ten minutes after the meeting finished a few of us were making our nightly visit to the Sun at Richmond for the final time before going to Heathrow the next day. We discussed the voluntary booze ban over a couple of cool lagers in the public bar and reached the decision it was probably the correct thing to do. After a couple more we were convinced it was going to benefit the team and our chances. The 'booze ban' had our support.

One of the boys arrived back at the Petersham Hotel just after 2.00 a.m., slightly tired and a little emotional, and seeing a light on in the team room he assumed it was a couple of squad members looking for food. So he climbed the stairs to the first floor and pushed open the door. He had just enough time to see the backs of Jack Rowell, Les Cusworth and Mike Slemen, the coaching team, studying a rugby video. In an instant the super-quick scrum-half reversed out of the doorway and ran to his room as the three of them turned in their seats to see a door wide open to the corridor.

Most of us were expecting a late start since we weren't leaving until mid-afternoon, so a 7.30 a.m. alarm call from Les Cusworth informing us of an emergency meeting was not welcome. Everyone was summoned to the team room where we found a stony-faced Jack Rowell. To say he wasn't happy goes nowhere near describing how angry he was. He'd had a few hours to think about the previous night's incident and had obviously decided someone was going to pay. I looked around the room and noticed most of the squad were looking bleary-eyed and confused, but they had nothing to worry about. One individual (who many years later won ITV's *Dancing on Ice* competition) appeared to be very anxious.

Jack got straight to the point.

'Someone has let the entire squad down,' he began. 'We had an agreement, an agreement amongst men, no one was going to drink alcohol for the next few weeks and within hours one of you is coming back to the hotel at 2.00 a.m., and I'm assuming the individual had not been out on a moonlight walk. If I find out who it was make no mistake they will leave this campaign immediately. In fact they will never play for England again while I'm in charge.'

He continued in this vein for a few minutes and it became apparent where most of it was being aimed. In fairness to Jack he never made any accusation, but the fact he looked at me more than anyone else was an indication of whom he thought might be the culprit. As did Martin Bayfield who was sitting behind me and leaned forward making a 'tut, tut, tut' sound near my ear.

Jack left the room in a fury and a few of the boys obviously suspected I might have been involved and uttered little comments like, 'Close one, Jase' and 'Got away with it again, Leonard'. All the time the 6ft 10in Martin Bayfield was looking down at me, continuing his tut tut tutting. I was beginning to feel guilty even though I knew it couldn't have been me. There were no members of the management left in the room as I said, 'It wasn't me,' with as much indignation as I could muster. 'It couldn't have been me, I didn't get in until 6 a.m.!'

Assuming he no longer has realistic aspirations of playing for England again, and for the benefit of overseas readers who have not been subjected to *Dancing on Ice*, the naughty boy Jack was referring to was a twenty-three-year-old Kyran Bracken, who went on to play in excess of fifty times for England. Might have been more if he'd followed my example.

Jetlagered

In 2003 the England team arrived in Perth, Australia, almost a month before the tournament kicked off, all part of Clive Woodward's professional approach to the campaign. He knew it would take a few days to recover from jetlag and decided there was no point in training until we were all fully acclimatised. As a result we were told we had three days off before we got down to business. To be fair we had trained incredibly hard for years and in particular the previous six months, so a bit of downtime was not going to affect our fitness levels. Clive suggested we spent the time relaxing and getting in sync with the Australian clock. He had a mature approach to alcohol and said he didn't mind if we went out for a couple of beers to help the process. That was all I needed to hear.

On the first night I took out all the young members of the squad for a couple of drinks. We had a great evening and I felt I'd managed to pass on some of my experience when I brought them all back to the hotel at about 4.00 a.m.

On the second night I took out the senior members of the squad, who proved they had more stamina than the younger lads by arriving back at 5.00 a.m.

On the third night I took out everyone and I like to think this was critical in helping the team bond (although having been together for several years there may be a limit to how tight a team can become). The vast majority (minus Jonny Wilkinson, of course, who was safely tucked up in bed) returned to the hotel at 6.00 a.m.

Day four and we have a 10.00 a.m. training session. I've had a couple of hours' sleep, a quick shower and am getting in the lift to go to breakfast. One floor down and the lift doors open to allow Clive Woodward to enter and join me. I am looking a little bit shabby, to say the least. Clive stares at me for a few seconds and says, 'Jase, you look absolutely shocking, are you okay?'

I raise my hand to my face and try to talk out of the side of my mouth in an attempt to divert the alcohol fumes away from him, 'Clive, I've never been affected this badly before but the jetlag is f****** killing me.'

Heaven is not a Place on Earth

Martin Bayfield

'Martin was a valuable member of the England team for several seasons; at 6ft 10in he often intimidated the opposition and dominated the line-out. He played thirty-one times for his country and in all three Lions Tests in New Zealand during the 1993 tour.

'Forced to retire from rugby due to injury in 1998, he developed another skill on the after-dinner speaking circuit. He is without doubt the best rugby speaker and probably one of the top three sporting speakers in the UK. He also entered the world of television presenting, including anchoring ITV's World Cup coverage in 2007 and also the *World's*

Strongest Man. Ironically his most famous role earned him little if any recognition, as Robbie Coltrane's body double during all the _Harry Potter_ films, where he played Hagrid, particularly in the longer shots when they needed to emphasise the size of the giant. He was delighted after the second film when his name appeared in the credits as an actor and not a stuntman!

'Our international careers overlapped for just a season or two during which time I thoroughly enjoyed his company, an extremely funny man who sees the humour in every situation.'

My only World Cup experience as a player came in the 1995 tournament. From an English perspective things went quite well on the field of play apart from that lad Jonah who did spoil things a bit. Off the field I was personally quite interested to see how relations between our coach Jack Rowell and a prominent figure in South African rugby, Louis Luyt, developed.

Jack Rowell was coach of the English team from 1994 to 1997 and during his time in charge England won twenty-one of their twenty-nine games, making him in 'percentage terms of games won' England's most successful coach. Prior to this he was head coach of the successful club side Bath, overseeing the glory years when for an extended period of time they appeared to be invincible, winning numerous Cup finals at Twickenham together with a collection of league titles. He was also a successful businessman who acted as chairman of a number of companies in the public and private sectors, predominantly in the food industry, including Dalgety plc, where he was executive director responsible for the consumer foods division. One other piece of information you will need to know about Jack is he has a razor-sharp wit, not always understood by all, but nevertheless great company in social situations. Given his background of success coupled with a healthy ego it was always going to be an interesting encounter when he met Mr Luyt, the President of the South African Rugby Union.

Louis Luyt has been described as a business tycoon and politician. He was a rugby player of some repute as a young man, and went on to found Triomf Fertiliser, Luyt Breweries, and also took control of the Ellis Park Stadium in Johannesburg, venue for the 1995 World Cup final. It's fair to say he was not overburdened with self-doubt. To be kind I would describe him as a confident man bordering on arrogant. Perhaps the following snippet of information will allow you to form your own opinion. After the 1995 World Cup final, there was a huge celebratory dinner. In a speech resonating with old Afrikaans conceit, Mr Luyt proclaimed the victorious Springboks as, 'The first "true" world champions. There were no "true" world champions in the 1987 and 1991 World Cups because South Africa was not there. We have proved our point.' This statement was described by the New Zealand media as 'boorish'. The inference clearly was that had South Africa been allowed to compete they would have won the previous two tournaments as well. When you consider New Zealand, the beaten 1995 finalists, were winners in 1987 it will not surprise you to learn that the All Blacks' captain

Sean Fitzpatrick walked out of the function, followed by his team.

One year prior to the World Cup, England took the opportunity to tour South Africa, allowing the squad to experience the country and some of the stadiums we'd be playing in during the tournament. It was seen as the perfect preparation for the team and it also brought Jack and Louis into contact for the first time. Both men had strong personalities, with Jack having the edge when it came to wit and repartee. At post-match functions both men often had to give a speech and without doubt Jack was the winner of these unofficial contests. You do not reach their respective positions without having a strong competitive streak.

Louis knew he was coming off second best and was heard saying to Jack that he was going to enlist the best scriptwriters in South Africa in order to produce a speech which would deliver all of Louis's aims, which in effect amounted to ensuring he looked good while making Jack look small (not an easy thing to do to a man who is over 6ft 6in tall). Jack took the news in good heart and smiled at Louis as if to say 'bring it on'.

Following our victory in the first Test, Louis was only too keen to get on his feet and deliver his talk, explaining how England had been lucky and that things would be different the following week. In retrospect it was not an improvement on previous efforts, with humility once again failing to secure a slot on the agenda. Jack was obviously delighted with our win and once again managed to turn the screw just another notch while on his feet. At the time the South Africans were developing an additional tier to a stand at Kings Park, Durban, and I recall Jack saying he felt the developers had missed a trick by not inviting Louis to each match and asking him to open his mouth, as this would easily provide space for the additional 15,000 seats they were seeking at very little cost. Seven days later we did in fact lose to South Africa and it was clear to everyone Jack was not best pleased with the result. He had a face like thunder for a couple of hours after the final whistle, but in true Jack style he became more upbeat as the evening wore on.

The post-match function was of the highest quality, something Jack covered in his speech. Everything was top-class, there was even a lady playing a harp in a corner of the room. Jack dealt with the more formal aspects early on by thanking South Africa for hosting a superb tour. He talked about the dinner itself and delivered a line which had the English team roaring with laughter in addition to those who didn't live in fear of Louis Luyt.

Jack was in full flow as he said, 'In terms of quality this is possibly the best dinner I've ever attended, I look at the fine bone china and notice it's of the highest standard, as is the cutlery and the crystal glass. The food has been exquisite and the wine some of the best I've ever tasted. The service has been first-class and the venue second to none. In fact a few minutes ago I looked around this magnificent setting and stored a mental image. I then closed my eyes and listened to the conversation and laughter and when I heard the harpist playing over to my right I honestly felt as though I was in heaven. I then opened my eyes, saw Louis Luyt, and instantly realised I couldn't have been.'

Another great victory for Jack.

1999

The 1999 Rugby World Cup was hosted by Wales and saw a change in the format, as for the first time the big eight nations did not qualify automatically. Only the champions, the runners-up, the third-place playoff winners from 1995 and the host nation were afforded that luxury. This meant South Africa, New Zealand, France and Wales were assured of their places, with sixty-five nations taking part in a new qualification process.

Another modernisation for the fourth Rugby World Cup was the expansion to a twenty-team format, divided into five pools of four, a scenario that necessitated a quarter-final playoff round involving the five runners-up and the best third-placed team to decide who would join the pool winners in the last eight.

England was once again in the same group as New Zealand and suffered a hefty 30–16 defeat, which meant that even with huge victories over Italy and Tonga (67–7 and 101–10 respectively), and notching up an impressive tally of twenty-two tries (none by me), we were confined to second place, and thanks to the new format a playoff match against Fiji. The game took place at Twickenham and although the Fijians were unlikely to pose too much trouble for the England team, the very fact of having to play the match created a major problem because the winner was due to take to the field again only four days later, for the quarter-final in Paris. The opposition would be a pool winner, in our case South Africa, who had avoided the playoff stage and therefore had a full nine days to prepare.

England beat Fiji 45–24 in a very physical match (again I failed to score) and departed for Paris. Having encountered the force of Jonah Lomu four years previously, it was to be another giant of the game that would send us home prematurely (if you are English, that is) this time. The stand-out performer in the quarter-final was the South African Jannie De Beer, who was transformed from 'occasional Springbok fly-half' to 'national hero' when he kicked a world-record number of dropped goals against us. De Beer had been second-choice in his position up to then, but an injury to Henry Honiball gave him the starting spot for our game. The match remained close until De Beer took control in the second half, slotting his five dropped goals, five penalties and two conversions to clinch (okay, walk away with) a 44–21 victory. As someone who played in the match, let me tell you his metronomic kicking was heartbreaking. Oh, and for the record, none of England's points were scored by me.

The semi-final ties brought the 1999 Rugby World Cup to

life. Though Wales was the tournament's designated host nation, matches were also played in England, France, Scotland and Ireland, with both semi-finals staged at Twickenham. Australia met South Africa in a gripping match, in which Jannie de Beer (who else?) had kicked five penalties and a dropped goal whilst Matt Burke had slotted over seven penalties for the Australians. With Australia leading 21–18 eight minutes into injury time, a Springbok defeat looked inevitable. However, in the last minute referee Derek Bevan awarded South Africa another penalty which de Beer successfully kicked (his sixth) to level the scores at full time.

The stalemate ensued until the third minute of the second period of extra-time, when from forty-five metres out Stephen Larkham catapulted Australia into the lead with the first, and possibly most important, dropped goal of his career (it was a mode of scoring that was becoming increasingly influential in World Cup tournaments). Burke then followed this up with his eighth penalty score of the game and Australia were through to their second Rugby World Cup final.

The second semi-final was staged the day afterwards, on Halloween, and it turned out to be a bit of a nightmare for the All Blacks. In a rerun of the 1987 final they were taking on France, and it appeared they had the game sewn up when they led by fourteen points in the second half. However, a few minutes after the restart France suddenly decided to go for it and produced some of the most amazing rugby I've ever witnessed. Christophe Lamaison dropped two goals and scored two penalties and then, with the deficit reduced to two points, Christophe Dominici collected a chip from Fabien Galthie to touch down for a try, converted by Lamaison. France now led 29–24 and this was stretched further when Richard Dourthe gathered a Lamaison kick and crossed the try line, Lamaison again converting. Six minutes before the final whistle Philippe Bernat-Salles added France's fourth try of the game, chasing the ball and beating the New Zealand wing Wilson to the line. Lamaison, almost inevitably now, converted, taking his personal points haul to twenty-eight. In this exceptional display by the French, New Zealand had conceded thirty-three points without reply until Wilson gained a consolation try in the last minute of the game. With the final score at 43–31 the jubilant French made their way into their second World Cup final and the New Zealanders once more returned home unexpectedly early.

Australia and France met at the Millennium Stadium for the eagerly anticipated final. France had been in this position once before and this would also be Australia's second final, having won the tournament in 1991. Following two glorious semi-final displays the match did not reach the heights set at Twickenham. The new Millennium Stadium was a fitting venue but unfortunately the pitch was well below World Cup standards and both teams appeared lacklustre, with Australia closing down the French play, prohibiting the freedom and free-flowing running rugby they had enjoyed against the All Blacks.

Australia won convincingly 35–12 in a one-sided match. Captain John Eales lifted the Webb Ellis Cup and Tim Horan deservedly received his recognition as Player of the Tournament, whilst the highly impressive Gonzalo Quesada of Argentina won the Golden Boot award, having scored a total of 102 points in the tournament.

There is an interesting historical footnote to the 1999 final. It took place on the same day, 6 November, as the referendum in Australia to determine whether the country should remain in the Commonwealth or become a republic. Many of the Australian players were keen to have their say and it was arranged for them to vote well in advance at the Ambassador's house in Dublin. John Eales was the first to emerge after registering his preference and faced a throng of eager journalists.

'So what do you make of all this John?'

'It would be interesting if we ended up playing England in the final and beat them, and the republic got up in the referendum.'

An innocuous and fair comment you would have thought, but before long whenever John was mentioned in the press in England he was described as 'Republican Captain John Eales . . .' I suspect John took all this in his stride, until perhaps the second before he was due to be presented with the Cup by Her Majesty the Queen. As it turned out, he needn't have worried as he explained to me over a beer one day.

'I remember thinking, I hope she doesn't read the papers. I don't know if she had read anything or not, but as she handed me the trophy she had a satisfied look on her face, perhaps indicating we'd both achieved what we wanted. On the front page of *The Times* the following day was a cartoon of the Queen handing me the trophy with the line, "Looks like we both defeated a Republic today."'

For the record, the no vote polled 55 per cent and Australia remained as they were.

If it perhaps lacked some of the emotion generated four years earlier, from a commercial point of view RWC 1999 once again broke all records, generating almost £50 million profit. It also demonstrated the growth in popularity of rugby union, as it was watched by a global television audience in excess of three billion. The sport was now big business and needed careful management.

A Few De Beers Too Many

The game has changed immensely in the last dozen years. In the modern era defences are now so much better that it is rare to see a back-row forward carry the ball any significant distance before being swallowed up by the opposition, whereas in the 1999 World Cup I seemed to get under a lot of high balls and go on a charge back up the field. In fact it became a spread bet option entitled 'Larry's Carries' with people betting on how many yards I would carry the ball. They also introduced 'Mehrtens' Metres' (the All Blacks fly-half) and the less well-named, but still popular, 'Lomu's

Yards'. Whilst I managed quite a few yards in earlier matches, sadly against South Africa in the quarter-final I was man-marked exceptionally well by their No. 8 Bobby Skinstad, who did a great job ensuring I didn't gain too much ground.

The other obvious difference in the past twelve years is technology. In the South African match their scrum-half, Joost van der Westhuizen, scored a try early on having clearly been in touch. With only the officials on the pitch able to make a judgement the score stood, whereas today the referee has the option of consulting a fourth official who has the benefit of TV replays if he's in any doubt regarding the validity of a try (just ask Mark Cueto!). I'm not making excuses, we lost, with Jannie De Beer magnificent as I said, but had that try been disallowed, things could have been different.

The entire team took the defeat very badly. We had not expected to leave the competition so early and genuinely thought we were in with a strong chance of winning. Everyone had prepared well, both mentally and physically. I think I'm correct in saying all the English players had voluntarily banned alcohol from our diets for several weeks prior to the start of the tournament. Need I say more about how seriously we took the whole affair? In fact, we were all feeling so desolate and numb that we didn't even go out for a beer after the match. That's the level of shock we were in. Scary. Still, you can't let things get you down for too long, especially when we realised it was likely to be the last time that particular squad was going to be together. Manager Clive Woodward was doubtless making preparations for

2003 (which seemed to go okay) and some of the older players were likely to be forced to take the long walk into the sunset.

So the following afternoon we hit the streets of Paris and decided it was time to have a drink and put the world to rights. Most of the squad were present, including all the Leicester players. Things were always a little more complicated when they were involved. It was a bit like pouring petrol onto a burning fire, anything could happen and it was probably going to be dangerous, not least because most of them had an egalitarian relationship with alcohol. All alcohol had to be treated equally, and therefore drunk in the same quantity as Ruddles beer. Potentially lethal if you're on a vodka run. Jonny Wilkinson was also involved and in all honesty it was the first and almost the last time I ever saw him drink (there was a sherbet or two consumed after the 2007 final). He was completely stitched up and in a bit of a mess by the end of it. Thinking back, he perhaps felt so dreadful afterwards that he made the decision there and then that alcohol was not going to play a significant part in his life, unlike the rest of us who have consistently managed to overcome that feeling regardless of how awful we feel.

Rather than drown our sorrows we decided to celebrate Joe Worsley, who had made his international debut against Tonga a couple of weeks earlier, and an Irish bar in St Germain was selected as the perfect venue from which to start things off. Everything was going well, the boys were swapping shirts, sweaters, even trousers with the locals and the beer was flowing. From there a few more bars enjoyed our patronage as we continued to drink and swap clothes that had already been exchanged several times before. I remember thinking if this carries on much longer we might end up getting our original gear back.

The afternoon drifted into the evening and onwards into the night and by 4.00 a.m. we'd reached the Champs-Elysées with its beautiful bars, cafés, luxury speciality shops and clipped horse-chestnut trees (all recalled from a subsequent trip, not from that night). To be honest, the troops did not match the surroundings, all very much the worse for wear, shuffling around in an eclectic selection of ill-fitting clothes. Even our leader and inspiration, Martin Johnson – I need to be careful here – was not shall we say as upright as he could have been. Indeed he seemed intent on inspecting the Parisian pavements from close quarters. As shocking as this next statement sounds, it was time for me to take responsibility, so I called to the one member of the England team who was still in the early stages of warming up, Jason Leonard, and told him we needed to get Johnno back to the hotel.

Jason stopped a cab as I used all my strength to assist my captain towards the rear doors. I will never forget the alarmed look on the poor cabbie's face as he repeated the words 'non, non, non', and Jason, who is practically fluent in 4.00 a.m. French, replied 'oui, oui, oui'. With both back doors opened to prevent the poor guy driving off, Jason pulled from one side and I pushed from the other and finally Johnno was safely wedged in. Jason then produced a card from his pocket,

Hotel Sofitel, near the Place de la Concorde, and gave it to the driver as I threw a decent number of francs onto the passenger seat. Mission accomplished, Jason looked at me with a satisfied expression on his face. 'Well done, Lol, he'll be all right now.' Obviously I have no idea what happened after the cab pulled away but Johnno was alive the next day, even though he looked like death.

Back inside the bar we found ourselves in conversation with Leon Lloyd and Neil Back, when a guy complete with the cross of St George painted on his face approached the group. Rather naïvely he decided it was the right moment to tell us in general, and Neil Back in particular, what he thought of England's performance. Now we can all take criticism, particularly when it's justified, but in the early hours of the morning during a bit of a session is probably not the best time to deliver it. We were still conscious of our responsibilities, however, and politely agreed it had not been the result we were hoping for.

That should have been that, but the guy then decided to inform Backy that not only was he a disgrace, but he also lacked passion, all the while stubbing his index finger into Neil's chest. I can only assume he thought it was safe to have a go at Backy because at 5ft 10in he didn't appear much of a threat. Schoolboy error. For the record, in my opinion very few people throughout the history of English rugby have played with more passion and desire than Neil Back. It came as a surprise therefore when Backy asked him to repeat what he'd said. Foolishly the bloke did so, and that's when Backy delivered his own personal, non-verbal, response from very short range. As the guy disappeared over the table behind him, Backy picked up his beer, held it in a very steady hand, smiled and muttered, 'I thought that's what he said,' before returning to the conversation as if nothing had happened.

Clive Woodward had become England's coach in 1997 and things started to move in the right direction from then, although probably not as quickly as Clive would have hoped. After a surprise defeat leading up to the tournament he was quoted as saying, 'Judge me on the World Cup performance.' A quarter-final defeat was not what he would have wished for, but there was enough support for him to remain in his job. And as we all know, the next four years proved to be very successful.

The Price of Success

Matt Perry

‘Matt’s a player I know well, we played many games together for England after he’d caught the eye of Clive Woodward during his time as Bath coach. He selected “Pezza” to make his debut in what was his first game in charge of England, against Australia in 1997. From a forward’s perspective he was a fantastic guy to play with as he would always get you playing on the front foot and establish a real target for you on the pitch. At the tender age of twenty-three he became England’s most capped full-back of all time (a record I believe he still holds) and would undoubtedly have gone on to establish an almost unassailable total had the rugby player’s curse not ruined the second half of his career. He sustained a back injury on the Lions

tour to Australia in 2001 (playing in all three Tests) which was the beginning of a catalogue of further injuries that eventually caused his early retirement in 2007.

'Pezza is a relatively quiet man, popular throughout the rugby world. He is one of the most modest and unassuming players I have ever met, blessed with immense ability. I sometimes wonder if he knew how good a player he was. He now works for a performance coaching and training consultancy in the South West.'

My only World Cup experience came in 1999. Injury, coupled I suppose with Clive Woodward failing to select me, ruled me out of the triumphant 2003 campaign. The frustrating thing for me was I knew it was going to be successful, or rather I knew the England team was going to have every chance of being successful, primarily due to the approach of our coach/manager Clive Woodward.

Clive was probably the first England coach who told the Rugby Football Union what he wanted. Those who had gone before him appeared to have resigned themselves to working with what they were given. I remember reading a story in Clive's book about his first day in the job, when he arrived at Twickenham to the surprise of many of the RFU hierarchy who wondered what he was doing there. Clive asked if they could point him in the direction of his desk. Clearly such a contraption was not something they felt Clive required, presumably thinking that he would initially be spending his time travelling the length and breadth of the country watching matches, followed by time on the training pitches coaching the squad he had scoured the nation to select. Let's just say Clive got his desk and it was the first of many battles he would win with the RFU in the years to come.

Clive wanted the very best for all his team; travel and accommodation were first class wherever possible, training facilities were the best available, as were all the coaches and support staff. By catering for virtually every need Clive effectively took away all the excuses. As players we only had ourselves to blame if things went wrong.

One of the innovations he brought to the squad was the introduction of laptops, with every player being provided with one before the 1998 tour to Australia. You'll appreciate this was in the relatively early days of the internet and long before broadband. It was Clive's intention to communicate with the players online, although I think it's fair to say some of the lads got far more use out of the solitaire and minesweeper games that came preloaded on the computers than from the hardware itself.

Clive told us that the team selected to play each match would be emailed to the individuals concerned and those not selected would be able to read the reasons why they had failed on that occasion to make the team. All the laptops originated in England, as did the host site for our email accounts, so it was necessary to log on in Australia via the UK in order to have Clive's messages sent back out to us. This clearly perplexed many of the players, the forwards in particular, with a number of the boys asking, 'Why can't he call a team meeting and tell us? After all, he's in the same bloody hotel!' Lessons were given in how to log on, not easy for someone like Jason Leonard, whose index finger would cover at least three keys on the keyboard, and with hindsight additional instruction in how to log off would have been invaluable. Many players either never shut down throughout the duration of the tour or at best remained logged on for hours on end. Younger readers will be interested to know this cost the RFU literally thousands of pounds when the telephone bill dropped through the letter box at Rugby House, Twickenham, a couple of weeks after the tour had ended (no inclusive packages in those days). Clive was possibly a bit too far ahead of the game with regard to technology in this instance, but in others he was spot on.

He identified the importance of the psychological approach to rugby. Within reason, the squads of all the major contenders for the World Cup were closely matched in terms of ability and fitness, so it was vital to work on the mental strength of the England team to try and eke an advantage over everyone else. It was because of all these innovations that I was so disappointed when my body started to fail me after playing for the Lions during the 2001 tour to Australia.

Clive was very good at making a player feel special. He knew when to have a private chat with individuals and when it was best to talk to the team collectively. Either way, my recollection is I felt better about myself and my ability as a rugby player after his inspirational words. But there was one occasion when his motivational chat perhaps went a little 'over the top', and caused a huge laugh in a team meeting.

In 1999 England were once again in the same World Cup group as New Zealand, and on the eve of the match we had our customary team meeting, at which Clive would run through all the last-minute details he believed would give us the edge. He spoke about the training we had done, he confirmed the game plan and discussed options if things were not going according to plan. I think I can speak on behalf of the squad when I say we all felt ready.

Everyone jokes about the All Blacks and how they manage to peak between World Cups and then fail to deliver when the tournament arrives. Clive was never going to entertain the thought of a poor New Zealand team, but he did use the opposition in that particular meeting as a way of inspiring the England squad. He had been standing at the front of the room as he spoke to us and to his right was what looked like a flip chart covered with a black drape.

Towards the end of the meeting he pulled off the drape and revealed a chart which had the England team selected to play the following day written down the left-hand side of the sheet, and on the right was the anticipated New Zealand team. He had started with the tight-head props and written the names in order of playing position, finishing with my position, No. 15, full-back. Both teams were lined up in this manner so you only had to glance to the right of your own name to see who your opposite number was.

After allowing us a few moments to look at both lists, Clive said he wanted to highlight something. 'Look at those teams and as you do I want you to know there is not one member of that New Zealand team who I consider good enough to gain selection for my England side.'

I think we all looked at the various match-ups and tended to agree; it certainly made you puff your chest out a little knowing Clive thought so highly of us. I picked out a couple of head-to-heads: Martin Johnson v Ian Jones – I'd have Johnno every time – and the same could be said when I spotted Will Greenwood up against Tana Umaga. However, there was one comparison we were all drawn to and it was left to Jason Leonard, who was sitting in front of me and next to Lawrence Dallaglio, to verbalise what every player in the room was thinking.

He leaned over to Lawrence and said in a stage whisper everyone could here, 'I don't know about you, Lol, but that 6ft 5in, 19st winger would get into my f****** side every day of the week.' The squad collapsed into laughter with the exception of Austin Healey, our winger, who was up against the All Black sensation Jonah Lomu the following day.

Target Rugby

Andrew Mehrtens

'When Andrew retired from international rugby he was New Zealand's all-time leading scorer with 967 points (since surpassed by Dan Carter). All Blacks rugby has had few players who have won such wide popularity and affection as Andrew. In a twelve-year career at first-class level he became a national figure rather than simply an icon of his Canterbury province. However, there was never total agreement on his ranking in the pecking order of All Black fly-halves. Some, headed by the legendary Colin Meads, believed Andrew was the best in his position ever produced by New Zealand. Others felt despite his immense skills, vision, kicking and ability to throw long cut-out passes to his centres and even

wingers, he had limitations. He was seen as lacking the physique or inclination to mix it physically, either taking the ball up or committing himself to the tackle. To be perfectly honest if I played outside half for the All Blacks and possessed the talent of Andrew Mehrtens I would expect my back row and centres to do *all* my tackling, allowing me to get on with being a genius.

'In 2005 he came over to the UK and had a very successful season with Harlequins before signing to French club Toulon, who gained promotion at the end of his first season. He is currently still playing in France for Béziers aged thirty-eight.'

My introduction to this project came as a result of a phone conversation with the 'great man' Lawrence Bruno Nero Dallaglio OBE.

The phone rings.

'Mehrts, it's Lawrence Dallaglio here, hopefully you can help me with a project I'm involved with. Is there any chance of getting a few World Cup memories from you, mate?'

'Hi, Lol, I'm fine, thanks for asking! No problem, I could talk about Rugby World Cups for three days without drawing breath. Tragically, during the entire three days I couldn't tell you what it's like to win a World Cup.'

'Don't worry about it, Mehrts, I've got that angle well and truly covered by a few of the England lads. Perhaps you can tell me what it's like to be a favourite every four years and then spectacularly fail to deliver!'

'Twat.'

The line goes dead. I've cut the 'gloating knob' off.

I do have a host of World Cup recollections and perhaps it would be useful to tell you a bit about 'setting goals' and the relevance of this approach to my World Cup experience. Throughout my career I have always set myself targets and worked as hard as I possibly could to achieve them. Long before I became an All Black, when playing my rugby for Canterbury I would stay on after training sessions and practise my goal kicking. On practically every occasion I would set myself a challenge. For instance I would need to successfully convert twenty consecutive kicks at goal from set places on the field before I could allow myself to go and get showered. Let me tell you, it's a real pain in the arse when you miss your eighteenth kick and have to start over again. However, establishing targets like this improved my performance and ultimately led to my selection for New Zealand.

My first experience of the World Cup as a player was in 1995 aged twenty-two. I was part of a squad including All Black legends Sean Fitzpatrick, Zinzan Brooke and Frank Bunce as well as a little-known player by the name of Jonah Lomu. Like every New Zealand team before, we only had one objective, to win the next match. It's a simple philosophy which throughout the history of All Blacks rugby has served us well, until the arrival of the World Cup.

Following the semi-final victory over England when Jonah ran in four tries (I'll repeat that, Lol, just in case it hasn't been mentioned previously). Following the semi-final victory over England when Jonah ran in four tries, we experienced the devastation of losing the final a week later against hosts South Africa, a 12–15 defeat after extra-time. Even though I was born in Durban, South Africa, and I appreciate the significance of that victory to the country and the creation of the Rainbow Nation, it does nothing to alleviate the pain of losing. To give you an indication of how deeply I felt the defeat, I changed the PIN code on my credit card to 1215 just to remind me of the hurt I felt when the final whistle was blown by referee Ed Morrison (before you even think about it, I changed my number again when I finished playing). Soon after the match I set myself a goal: 'I am never again going to be involved in a team which loses a World Cup final.'

Ask yourself this, is it possible to set a goal, do all you can to achieve it, realise the goal and then know you have failed in your objective? This sounds slightly confusing but if you read it slowly it will make sense.

The answer is yes, it is possible. So from 1995 through to 1999 I did all I could to improve my own performance and to assist the All Blacks in their desire to win the World Cup in the United Kingdom.

The tournament arrived and on 3 October 1999 we took our first step towards winning the trophy with a convincing 45–9 victory over Tonga in the pool stage. Twenty-eight days later on 31 October I achieved my goal of not being involved in a team which lost a World Cup final, when New Zealand lost 31–43 to France at Twickenham in the semi-finals! Having been 24–10 up courtesy of a couple of tries from Jonah we appeared to be cruising towards the final, when France, as only France can, suddenly turned on the style and scored thirty-three unanswered points before our winger Jeff Wilson got over the line for a consolation at the death. As the French revival grew I remember seeing and hearing thousands of English fans join with their French counterparts in singing 'Allez Les Bleus' (and I thought it was the Aussies the Pommies despised).

As you can see I achieved my goal without achieving any success. I needed to rethink in order to rule out any possibility of defeat. Before long I had it. My new goal was set. 'Never to be part of a team that loses a World Cup match.'

Once again I spent a four-year period training and practising even harder to realise my goal. And four years later the Rugby World Cup arrived in Australia and I finally succeeded in achieving my goal. I was not involved in a team that lost a World Cup match, because I was not involved in the World Cup. The All Blacks had decided to drop me for the 2003 season only to recall me again in 2004. Once again I achieved my goal whilst failing to reach my objective.

Still, we are on home soil later this year and even though I will be sat in an armchair watching the matches, my hope will be the All Blacks have set themselves a goal – To WIN the World Cup. No ambiguity there.

2003

The Rugby World Cup organisers tinkered once again with the qualification and group stage structure in 2003. All teams reaching the quarter-final stage of the 1999 tournament were rewarded with automatic entry to the 2003 competition. This left twelve remaining places which were sought after by eighty-one nations from five continents, who fought it out in a qualification process which started three years before the opening game. For this tournament it was decided to have four groups of five teams competing in the pool stages, with the top two in each group progressing to the knockout stages. There was also the opportunity to earn a bonus point if a team scored more than four tries in a match or if a losing team was within seven points of the opposition at the final whistle.

Many people forget the 2003 RWC was originally awarded to Australia and New Zealand. However, a contractual dispute over ground advertising signage between the New Zealand Rugby Football Union and Rugby World Cup Limited meant

Australia were gifted the sole right to host the event. Apparently RWC Ltd wanted completely clean stadia so they could display RWC sponsors exclusively. The New Zealand RFU declared they could not comply with these wishes as they had pre-existing contracts with non-World Cup sponsors, a stance which eventually resulted in the tournament being taken away from New Zealand. I think it fair to assume RWC Ltd flexed their muscles over this, and in so doing left all future bidding countries well aware of the sponsorship requirements.

England were favourites with the bookmakers having consistently defeated South Africa, Australia and New Zealand during the previous eighteen months, home and away. Even so it was hardly plain sailing. The quarter-final against Wales saw us go into the changing rooms at half time 10–3 down and very much on the back foot. The introduction of Mike Catt in the second half took the pressure off Jonny Wilkinson and seemed to reinvigorate the backline, producing a much more confident performance that saw England progress to the semi-finals with a 28–17 victory.

Australia had little trouble reaching the same stage, but a semi-final against rivals and neighbours New Zealand was always going to be their sternest test. A 22–10 victory, during which they were never behind, proved they were up for the challenge and with home advantage many people started to believe they could win the World Cup for a third time in four tournaments. The other semi guaranteed a northern hemisphere side in the final as England took on France. Rain fell all day and by the time the match kicked off it had reached almost monsoon proportions. With France there is always the chance they can turn on the style and devastate you, but at the same time they are often accused of not being the best travellers. Finding themselves on the other side of the world in torrential rain was unlikely to suit their style of play, and so it turned out. England secured their place in the final with a 24–7 victory, with all their points coming from Wilkinson's boot.

It goes without saying the 22 November 2003 will be a date and a moment etched in my brain for ever. The England side had a huge amount of confidence and probably felt as though things were going according to plan when we found ourselves leading 14–5 at half-time. As all followers of rugby will know, the second half was very tense, ending in the eightieth minute with Elton Flatley kicking a penalty to level the scores at 14–14. Having spoken to numerous supporters back in England who watched the game on television, the impression I have is the majority of them could hardly bear to watch the two periods of extra-time. I have to tell you, from a player's perspective we were calm, genuinely calm. Martin Johnson and Clive Woodward said a few words and one or two of the senior players chipped in with a bit of advice and motivation, and that was it. We didn't need anything more. I can honestly say the thought we might lose never entered my head and I know this was the same for the rest of the team. We weren't arrogant, but we did have absolute belief in each other. We knew how hard we'd all worked to reach that stage of the tournament. To lose was not an option. So ironically, the calmest place to be was on the pitch, until Jonny's drop goal and the final whistle and then ... it all went crazy.

Unforgettable

The 2003 World Cup has been well documented, but here are some interesting and amusing behind-the-scenes stories which I hope are of interest.

Going into 2003 we were the No. 1 ranked team in the world and confidence was high. Clive had looked at every facet of the game. Our training, preparation, recovery, even transport and accommodation, everything, had been designed to give the team the best opportunity to achieve our goal of lifting the World Cup. Anything which could potentially provide us with an advantage was considered. The design of our kit was revolutionary, we had an 'eye coach' to improve peripheral vision, and somewhere along the way some bright spark had decided the most efficient way for the human body to recover from strenuous exercise was to sit in an ice bath for fifteen minutes (gee, thanks). It's a cliché, but no stone had been left unturned. We would only have ourselves to blame if we failed.

Unlike the situation discussed in a number of the 1987 stories, when teams arrived only a few days before the start of the tournament, in 2003 we arrived nearly four weeks in advance of the opening ceremony. In addition, we had actually visited Perth, where our campaign began, four months earlier. We had been on tour in the southern hemisphere and following the final match, a victory against Australia, Clive decided we were going to spend a few days there in order to acclimatise to the hotel, training facilities and surrounding area. Most people just wanted to get home but it was not negotiable. Would we have won the World Cup without the advance visit? No one can say, but it illustrates Clive's thorough approach and his desire for England to be the best-prepared team in the tournament.

Talking of Clive, it became obvious to all the players, particularly when we reached the knockout stage, that he always liked to be the final person to board the team bus. Hundreds, perhaps thousands of supporters used to converge on the team hotel and form a funnel from the hotel entrance to the bus which would be taking us to training or matches. Once we'd picked up on this fact one or two of us (okay, Leonard and myself) decided to do our best to mess up his routine. I'm sure his actions had nothing to do with adulation, and so I only mention in passing that when Clive was the last member of the England staff to leave the hotel all the cheers and applause from the gathered crowd were naturally directed solely at him.

It was Jason who came up with the plan. Before most training sessions and every match, the squad and coaching staff would have a private meeting in the hotel to clarify our aims and objectives for the day. After one such meeting Clive, Jason and I were the last three people to leave the room and as we walked down stairs towards the foyer, Jason theatrically clasped his forehead with his hand and gasped, 'Oh bollocks! I've only gone and left my boots in the meeting room.' He then looked at Clive and said, 'I'll run back and get them, you two go on ahead. I'll see you on the bus.' Clive and I continued down the stairs and had just reached the ground floor when, incredibly, Clive suddenly remembered something he needed to organise with the hotel reception. Who'd have thought? 'You go on ahead, Lol, I'll be there in a minute.'

I carried on to the bus and waited to see which of the other two would be the next to arrive. It was Jason and as he boarded he looked at me with a cheeky schoolboy grin. 'Is he on yet? Have we f***** him up?' I had to tell him what had happened in reception and then explained to the rest of the boys what we'd tried to do. A couple of minutes later Clive emerged, complete with a brilliant 'royal wave' as the England fans cheered his every step. He must have wondered what the hell was going on as he took his seat at the front, still waving to the adoring fans, with the rest of the bus pissing themselves with laughter.

I mentioned this to Clive a couple of years ago. 'Most members of the squad tried at some point or another to be the last person on the bus and you always managed to defeat us. It was a standing joke virtually every day for three weeks. It can't have been a coincidence.' To this he replied, 'Well, if it helped team morale all well and good, but I can assure you it was not intentional on my part.' My response to that? 'Bollocks.'

Closing in on fulfilling an ambition affects people in different ways. For example, as we progressed through the tournament there was no noticeable change in the demeanour of Martin Johnson. He was as bright, cheery and frivolous as ever. Conversely, you could tell Clive was getting increasingly animated the deeper into the competition we progressed. This was perhaps most notable following our 24–7 semi-final victory over France. Clive had organised a meeting for every playing member of the squad, which we assumed would involve some kind of debrief, looking at all the positives and identifying weaknesses we could work on in the coming days. Nothing strange in that, except for the fact that such meetings normally took place the day after a match. On this occasion Clive had called us together immediately and as the French game had been an evening kick-off, this meant we were gathering in the hotel sometime after midnight.

Clive launched straight into it. 'You are all on the verge of greatness. We've come through so much in the past few years I don't want us to mess it up so close to the finishing line. This means I don't want to see anyone discussing any of these commercial deals I keep hearing about. No book, no columns, nothing. I need you all to focus fully on the task in hand.' He continued in a similar vein for several minutes, and whilst I understood where he was coming from and what he was saying, I couldn't help thinking that surely there is a time and a place for this, and it isn't now. Clive, I said to myself, we've just beaten France, how about a couple of hours off, a decent sleep and get on with the job tomorrow? Albeit briefly, I honestly think Clive had lost the plot.

As I left the room I met one of Clive's good friends, a guy called Paul Monk, and told him to go and have a word as Clive appeared to be approaching meltdown mode. Paul entered the meeting room and the first person he encountered was Johnno, who was not in the mood for visitors. 'I don't know who you are but you're not allowed in the team room.' Paul responded by pointing at Clive. 'I'm the person who's going to speak to that bloody lunatic to try and calm him down.' 'Oh,' said the England captain, 'on you go then, mate. And good luck.' I assume the chat had the desired effect as Clive was much calmer the following day.

If I had to choose one single moment from the 2003 World Cup experience it would be that semi-final against France. As I ran onto the pitch the English support was truly amazing, huge swathes of white shirts all around the stadium creating an unbelievable atmosphere. The match was my sixty-fourth international for England and even though there had been many memorable matches before, not least my first cap, nothing came close to equalling the positive energy I experienced that evening. To succeed you need a decent team and confidence in your own abilities and in those of the players around you, but that day I realised just how important the support of a crowd is in helping to determine the outcome of a match. What hair I had on my neck was genuinely raised as I emerged under the floodlights for that match. It was an unforgettable experience.

As for the final, apart from the obvious, two memories will stick with me for ever. And both occurred before a tackle was made or a ball kicked. The first came as we walked out on to the pitch and I saw the Webb Ellis Cup standing proudly on display. It gave me a strange feeling. It was physically so close, but I knew there was a lot of effort and emotional expenditure required before its destination was determined. I'm not a particularly superstitious person but I refused to touch it. I didn't want to tempt fate.

The second happened almost immediately afterwards, when I looked up and saw Martin Johnson standing next to the Australian captain George Gregan. There was only one of those two men I wanted as my leader. I mean no disrespect to Gregan at all, he was an exceptional player and brilliant captain, but just from a physical perspective, Johnno at 6ft 7in and nearly 19st seemed indestructible. George was 5ft 8in and weighed in at less than 13st. He looked like a schoolboy in comparison to Johnno. To me it was further proof that England were going to win, and we did. But you know that already.

Deflating the Bus's wheels

Josh Lewsey

'Josh won his first England cap on the "Tour from Hell" to Australia in 1998, aged twenty-one. The vast majority of players from that tour never appeared in an England shirt again after a 76–0 defeat at Brisbane. It's a credit to Josh, and an indication of his determination to succeed, that he was not one of those lost souls.

'On the rugby front he was capped fifty-five times, scored twenty-two tries, and also toured with the Lions in 2005. His try count demonstrates his attacking ability, but as a forward I was always impressed by his defensive qualities. I knew any high ball was going to be fielded by Josh and returned with interest. At 5ft 10in and weighing less than 14st (89kg) he was not the biggest full-back I played with but it was extremely rare any attacker managed to get round him. Like me, his rugby highlight was winning the World Cup in 2003.

'Since retiring from international rugby Josh made an ascent of Mount Everest, falling just 100 metres short of the summit when he experienced problems with his breathing apparatus and was forced to descend. Having been so close I asked him why he hadn't just sprinted to the top, taken a photo and clambered back down. Josh patiently explained that at such altitude a good rate of progress was about three steps a minute (Jason Leonard's top match-day speed) and the temperature was so low one of the guys he was climbing with was forced to turn back when the covering of his eyes (the corneas) froze. Not that I needed it, but that and other tales confirmed to me what a tough and gritty competitor Josh is.'

No matter how many times a player represents his country he will always experience a healthy dose of nerves leading up to a match. All international matches feature prominently in a player's mind, but it's fair to say none more so than a World Cup final.

When you go to bed on the eve of a match your brain is full of thoughts, predominantly concerning the game, the team performance and your own personal contribution. The combination of nerves and an overactive mind often means sleep is hard to come by. So to counteract this, the England medical team have for many years supplied a sleeping pill called Zopiclone to ensure a good night's sleep before a game. It's entirely up to each individual whether they take the pill or not, and as a generally relaxed person I tended to accept one but very rarely needed to use it. Players who took them always said how well they'd slept and never felt drowsy the following day, but I was always worried I'd be the exception and feel lethargic and sluggish. So the night before the final, I went to bed as usual, read for a while to clear my mind and managed a fairly decent sleep.

The following day was filled with team meetings, relaxation periods, in fact anything to while away the hours before the 8.00 p.m. kick-off. To be honest there was nothing to be said or done which would have made any difference; we were as ready as we were ever going to be, just waiting for the first whistle.

Fast forward to Jonny's drop goal, referee Andre Watson blowing the final whistle and England are world champions, the first (and so far only) northern hemisphere side to achieve the feat. It doesn't get much better than that – time to celebrate!

I remember returning to the team hotel at 11.00 a.m. the following morning with a couple of team-mates, thinking to myself, Well done, Josh, you've been out all night and absolutely 'smashed it' and you are still managing to walk. Being fit has an added benefit when it comes to celebrating: you can drink a huge amount of alcohol without feeling completely out of it. It was therefore something of a personal comedown to discover I obviously wasn't as fit as most of the other players, who didn't arrive back until 4.00 p.m., the time we were due to depart en masse to the International Rugby Board awards dinner.

Following the do several of us pushed straight on through the next night, continuing our party. There were more beers, more English supporters to talk to and a few Aussies who had to accept some gloating on our part. I knew it was all going to end at some point but was doing all I could to ensure I played my part in proceedings. As a consequence I once again arrived back at the hotel around noon (Monday), in time to pack my bags and get ready for the flight home later the same day.

We all arrived at the airport and a few of us had a 'cleansing beer' before boarding. I am now officially 'ruined'. I'd been running on fumes for well over sixty hours and needed to board the British Airways flight, find my seat, get comfortable and sleep all the way home. It was at this point I received some potentially alarming news: the boarding passes, and therefore the seat allocations, had all been issued in alphabetical order, Phil Larder (our defence coach), Josh Lewsey and JASON LEONARD! I'm sure other players have contributed stories featuring Jason Leonard OBE but all you really need to know for the purpose of my story is that sixty hours of drinking for Leonard is little more than a warm-up. Having spent the last few days on the 'launch pad', he was doubtless getting ready for 'take-off' both figuratively and literally. My only hope was to be at the front of the boarding queue, get to my seat and fall into a deep, unconscious sleep. Seconds after I found my seat I saw Leonard ('Fun Bus') wandering down the aisle, studying his boarding card and looking at the seat numbers below the overhead lockers.

A broad smile appeared on his face when he saw the vacant

seat to my right. 'Ah, Josh me old mate, you'll have a little drink with your uncle Jase, won't you?' I vividly remember thinking, Oh dear God please don't do this to me. I looked around for players who would swap with me, they either ignored my gaze or gave me the 'rather you than me' look. I was on my own.

'Come on, Josh, let's crack on. What do you want to start with, a beer, a drop of white or something stronger?' I was feeling close to death and knew a few hours with the Fun Bus would cause further short-term damage and probable long-term health problems. I needed a way out.

'It's okay, Jase, I'm a bit tired and need to get a bit of sleep.' I even tried a bit of lame humour: 'I want to be looking my best when we all meet the Queen on Wednesday.'

'Don't be silly, Josh, you know it makes sense, my son, have a little drink with your old mucker Jase. Tell you what, I'll organise a nice claret to get us going.'

Within minutes of take-off we both had a glass of red wine in our hands, with one of us doing all the talking and the other (needless to say, me) not. It's difficult to convey how tired I was. Days of virtual non-stop drinking on top of the exertion of a World Cup tournament had all caught up with me. The last thing I needed was an extended session with Leonard and that's when it hit me: there was a way out. It would take the smallest of efforts on my part to guarantee a quiet trip home. I reached into the overhead locker and took out my flight bag and removed my 'stash'.

Initially, I intended to take one of my Zopiclones myself, but in reality I didn't need it. All my body craved was sleep. And that was precisely what it wasn't going to get. It would take falling into a virtual coma before Leonard would stop pestering me. I decided I needed to take positive action and surreptitiously slip Jase a Mickey. A single Zopiclone is normally sufficient to put a grown man out for a solid eight to ten hours, so when Leonard's attention was diverted briefly by Phil Larder I dropped one into his red wine and waited for it to take effect. During the next few minutes he finished his drink and with the words, 'Josh, keep up, son, you're slacking,' he poured us both another glass. At the first opportunity, I slipped another tablet into his fresh glass, realising the mistake I had made. I wasn't attempting to subdue a mere mortal man, I was trying to knock out an elephant.

It took a total of three and a half tablets before I finally tranquillised the bastard. I was so desperate I actually didn't care if I killed him, I just needed to be left alone to get some rest. The end arrived somewhere over Perth and things happened really quickly; he took a deep breath, stuffed a bread roll into his mouth and that was it. Just prior to following him into the deepest sleep of my life I have a vague recollection of a few members of the public who were on the flight taking photographs of the unconscious Jason Leonard enjoying what could have been his final meal before going to meet his Maker.

Dear diary

Shane Byrne

'Whilst a very good hooker who played forty-one times for Ireland from 2001 to 2005, Shane Byrne will always be remembered by the public for his hairstyle (or lack of it, style that is, not hair). Born twenty years too late for his mullet to be fashionable, if indeed it ever was, it never seemed to bother him and no amount of ribbing from team-mates and opposition would persuade him to change it.

'On the rugby front he was a robust player with good mobility and according to members of the England front row I've talked to, an awkward customer in the set pieces, often making things uncomfortable for opposition front rows. In effect he did exactly what he was meant to and very well

too. He also played in all three Tests in New Zealand for the Lions in 2005.'

From 2002 to the end of 2003 I did something I had never previously done. I kept a diary. So when Lawrence asked me to contribute some World Cup memories for his book, I dusted off the diaries and realised as I read through the entries the information recorded would provide an insight into the life of a professional rugby player leading up to a World Cup and during the campaign itself.

It was a hell of a long road for the Irish side to get to Australia, and also one of the best experiences of my life. It started in August 2002 with pre-qualifying training. Ireland had failed to reach the quarter-final stage of the previous tournament following a terrible loss to Argentina, so we had to qualify for 2003. After a warm-up game in Limerick against a strong Romanian side we headed off for our first qualifier, against Russia. This required an incredible trip to a place called Krasnoyarsk in central Siberia. To give you an idea of the size of Russia, Dublin is closer to Moscow than Moscow is to Krasnoyarsk. We comfortably won a hard-fought match, only to have to rush all the way back to Dublin for a home fixture against Georgia four days after our return from the Siberian wastes. We had to travel further for our home match than the away team! (Someone needs to look at the scheduling of qualifying matches.) Victory against Russia and Georgia secured our qualification and also provided us with the platform to continue the year with some great victories, including the highlight of my career when we defeated Australia in the autumn. By the time we played England in the 2003 Six Nations Grand Slam decider we had won a record ten consecutive matches (sadly it was not extended to eleven).

After the Six Nations we had a training camp every two weeks to keep our minds on the job, followed by a tour of Australia, Tonga and Samoa which, let me say, was a severe physical test. Tonga and Samoa may not be the most technically gifted of sides in international rugby but they certainly know how to knock 'seven shades of shit' out of you for eighty minutes. After the tour we finally had some holiday (a whole two weeks off). Since the birth of my twin girls in October 2002 I had been home for eight days in a row only twice. Our final run-in towards the 2003 World Cup was a training camp in Poland, a training camp in Limerick, a training camp in Athlone, warm-weather training in Bilbao, Spain – where it rained all the bloody time – and then warm-up matches against Wales, Italy and Scotland.

During this build-up we had some motivational speeches from some amazing characters including 'Marvellous' Marvin Hagler, the undisputed World Middleweight Champion throughout most of the eighties, and the well-known adventurer and explorer Sir Ranulph Fiennes.

Marvellous was some creature, probably one of the greatest all-round boxers in recent history, and believe me he had no problem in telling us that. With a very level head he extolled the virtues of 'starving the doubt' and 'feeding the faith'. Although I understood the sentiment, I'm still not entirely sure how you actually achieve this. Anyway, this strategy obviously worked somewhat better for him than it did for the Irish team.

Sir Ranulph was a completely different experience. Throughout his career he has tended to attempt things that had not been done before, taking routes no one else has entertained or embarking on expeditions without any support other than the equipment and food he could carry or drag on a sledge. To be honest he could have spoken to us about tiddlywinks and made it sound interesting, but what a nutter. Five months before talking to us he'd had a double heart bypass operation and a couple of months later he successfully completed seven marathons on seven continents in seven days. I don't think I could have quite managed that. My biggest difficulty being that I didn't even know there were seven continents. Other than that ...

With all the intensive training and motivational assistance now complete we left for Australia on 29 September, landing in Sydney on 1 October where we were given one day to get over the trip and the jetlag (not enough time, in case you're interested). The travel seemed to affect some people worse than others. We thought Victor Costello might have been a casualty following a briefing on the local wildlife when we heard him ask Keith Gleeson, 'So what colour is the Australian Brown snake?' All the locals were very friendly with most claiming to have family connections to Ireland, even if it was only as a result of owning an Irish Terrier. It was pleasing to hear the Irish pool games were some of the hottest tickets for this stage of the tournament.

All of our World Cup matches were well documented at the time, so perhaps I can enlighten you regarding some of the things the boys did during their downtime. On one particular occasion we were offered a variety of options. We could climb the Sydney Harbour Bridge (why would you want to do that?). Go to the horse racing at Gosford (something I was tempted to do when I heard it was Ladies Day). Or visit the set of the Aussie soap *Home and Away* (just try and keep me away). What we didn't realise was that this seemingly innocuous trip was to be responsible for a major revelation. One that shook many of the squad to their very core. It transpired that scrum-half Peter Stringer was a massive fan of the TV show. He knew all the character names, the back stories, the actors who played them and much more besides. This was a man who had been entrusted to make split-second decisions on the pitch. It was very worrying.

Donncha O'Callaghan provided my personal highlight of the day when we were observing the filming of a scene taking place in a living room. On the coffee table was a large bowl of fruit and between takes, Donncha would sneak in and remove one piece of fruit at a time. I know it's not clever, but when every waking hour seems to be filled with rugby, rugby, rugby, watching a bowl of fruit slowly disappear, knowing it will be broadcast across the world in a few weeks' time, seemed hilarious to me.

Following my exciting visit to *Home and Away*, on the next occasion we had some time to ourselves I decided to go scuba diving, having qualified a couple of years earlier. Just before the dive I asked my usual question of the guide.

'Any sharks out there?'

'Yes.'

'WHAT?!! That's not the right answer – you're supposed to lie.'

Seeing the genuine look of fear on my face the instructor tried to save the situation by telling me he had never seen one on this particular dive and I'd have more chance of getting killed by a coconut than a shark. He obviously thought I was an idiot. I knew there were no coconuts under the water but there might be a f****** shark! I carefully made my descent, and was more vigilant than at any time in my life. The growing fear inside me was compounded when Mal O'Kelly cut his foot. Bright red blood flowed freely from the wound, which is surely tantamount to the ringing of a dinner bell to any shark within a twenty-mile radius? I made an instant decision, and left the water as fast as I could, leaving the lanky eejit O'Kelly to fend for himself. I'd seen *Jaws* after all.

By the way, many people have asked me over the years why one of my nicknames is 'Mullet'. Actually that's a lie, no one has ever asked, but I bring it up because during the tournament a team-mate brought to my attention that I had been very well supported in a fans' poll conducted by a prominent rugby website. At last, my skills had been properly recognised. Looking around the hotel reception I noticed an Irish supporter drinking coffee and tapping away on a laptop. I wandered over and asked if he minded me using it for a moment to check something. After making me agree not to visit any porn sites he remained close by as I typed in the address my team-mate had given me. With both of us staring at the screen, my face appeared (not a bad photo in my opinion) with the caption underneath reading: 'In a recent poll taken by our readers, Shane Byrne has been voted as having the sixth worst hairstyle in world rugby [wait for it . . .] *of all time.*' My new friend immediately bookmarked the page and no doubt sent it to all his mates shortly afterwards. The only saving grace was Brian O'Driscoll had come in eighth (I think he was going through his peroxide period at the time). I have never been under any illusion when it comes to the looks department but dear old Brian always reckoned he was something of a dish, and this poll obviously had an effect on him. If you look at any photo of Brian O'Driscoll from the end of the World Cup 2003 to the current day you will see a very sensible and presentable non-offensive hairstyle (vain bastard).

Wherever we went in Australia the local cops were great. They told us that whenever the Irish arrived in town (any town) and started to drink the place dry there was a marked reduction in the amount of crime. When we were in Melbourne they invited anyone interested to their shooting range. The guns they had were amazing, with my personal favourite being the .44 Magnum, straight out of *Dirty Harry*. I have a vivid memory of our prop forward John Hayes staring down the range at the target saying, 'Do ya feel lucky, bullseye? Well? Do ya?' Oh it felt lucky all right – John didn't get within an ass's roar of the target let alone the bullseye. Still, the trip was another great distraction from the rugby and finished without any major incident.

Looking back through my diary I notice Monday 3 November was a compulsory fun day.

Eddie O'Sullivan (coach) had decided to give us a full day of leisure. We called it a compulsory day of fun because although we were given the day off we had to get out of the hotel and do something; 'just chilling' was not on the agenda. The options were golf (too energetic), zoo (nah), aquarium/shark dive (once is enough, thank you), helicopter ride (interesting), but most of us, being big kids, went for go-karting.

I must say it was great craic, particularly as the guys in control gave us loads of time on the track and appeared to turn a blind eye as the boys broke all the rules, perhaps the most significant of which was also the most basic: all karts are to be driven in the same direction on the course. This was disregarded inside three laps by most of the forwards, who felt it was more of a challenge to avoid the oncoming traffic and also because it offered the additional pleasure of seeing the petrified faces of the backs as we forwards headed straight for them, playing our own high-speed game of 'chicken'. Malcolm O'Kelly had a fixation with a dummy standing in amongst the tyres on the side of the track, wearing orange dungarees and holding a chequered flag. At least I hope it was a dummy as O'Kelly managed to hit it twice, leaving it prostrate in the middle of the track in the way of oncoming drivers (from both directions). I think it is also worth noting that when all the laps were complete and most of the karts broken, I was declared the winner. It seems all my years of rallying up in the Tinnakilly Woods in my Uncle Dudley's car had finally paid off (Jeez, I hope he doesn't read this).

One final trip the management organised for us was to a wine chateau (or Aussie equivalent). Apparently Melbourne is near one of the big wine-growing regions of Australia, so after an exceptionally hard training session, we were ordered onto the team bus for an hour and a half journey to 'Chateau Billabong' or something similar. On arrival we were provided with some sustenance, a few plates of namby-pamby finger food which was of use to neither man nor beast. The signs were not encouraging. Following this we were taken on the 'exciting' tour where we learned how each particular vine thrives in the special soil, which helps produce the lurvely taste etc., etc., etc. (zzzzzzz, let's get on to the tasting/drinking portion of the day). Walking into another barn we were informed this was where the 'plink' was added to 'plonk' to produce a stunning sparkling red wine. Ah, sparkling red wine, I'll have a taste of that. This was when it was explained that no players were allowed any alcohol. For f**** sake, there was another four hours before we left the place and all we had to look forward to was watching the management 'taste' their way to oblivion. To make things worse it was Melbourne Cup day at the races. Why couldn't they have taken us there for some compulsory fun? By now, what little brain our loose-head prop Marcus Horan had previously laid claim to was in meltdown. Standing next to the vineyard owner looking out over 100 acres of vines, he said, 'So all those lines of big twigs are what you call grape trees?' 'Yes, that's right, grape trees,' the boss-man replied and walked silently away.

For the record, as a team we trained extremely hard almost every day. I have just highlighted the downtime in my ramblings here, which believe me are far more interesting than hearing about team tactics, shuttle runs and stamina sessions. That would have been even worse than finding out about the acidity of the earth in the Melbourne grape-growing region.

Spectator Sport

David Trick

'David Trick helped me with my last book *Rugby Tales* and again with this one. He finished his career as I started mine so we never played against each other. He reliably informs me he was bloody brilliant although the stats don't necessarily bear that out.

'He spent twelve seasons playing for the famous Bath club and has recently been elected President of Bath Rugby. He tells me he is honoured by the appointment but somewhat embarrassed as he's still thirty years short of his eightieth birthday and doesn't currently possess a blazer with red wine and food stains on the lapels! If I know Tricky, it will not be long before he does. On a serious note, he played 247 times for the club

and scored an amazing 171 tries, he also played twelve times for England at different levels, scoring eleven tries, which I'm sure you'll agree is some achievement. When researching the validity of these facts and figures (I gave him a ring to ask if they were true) all he could say was defences were pretty poor in his day, and this fact coupled with his exceptional pace on the wing and a huge fear of pain meant he was able to cross the try line on a number of occasions.

'As he assisted in the gathering of stories for this book he decided to write one of his own even though he never played in a World Cup. He did however travel to Australia for the 2003 tournament and recollects an incident in a local restaurant after our quarter-final against Wales.

'While I remember – Tricky, many thanks for your help.❞

Everyone remembers what happened in 2003, but that doesn't mean it isn't worth spelling out once again. England won the World Cup following an extra-time dropped goal from the 'boy wonder' Jonny Wilkinson. Whilst that moment remains my favourite on-field memory, off the field I will never forget an incident after the England–Wales quarter-final at the Suncorp Stadium, Brisbane.

I was part of a supporters' group from the UK and had arrived in the city a couple of days before the quarter-final stage of the competition. Having followed the Lions two years earlier in Australia I thought I had a reasonable idea of what to expect in terms of crowds and vocal support, but nothing I had experienced came close to the atmosphere before the Wales match on the evening of 9 November 2003. The narrow streets around the stadium were a sea of red and white with every bar and restaurant crammed full of passionate supporters, all confident of success (well the ones in white were). I was about a hundred yards from the ground and it took me the best part of twenty minutes to even get close to the entrance. All around were groups of varying sizes, drinking excessively, singing and chanting. It reminded me of one of the reasons I like rugby so much, thousands of fans from both teams in the same area, and not a hint of trouble.

I went into the stadium about half an hour before kick-off, ready to savour the atmosphere. A couple of minutes later the occupant of the seat to my right arrived. It was one of those occasions when you know the face but can't put a name to it. The only clue I had was he was wearing red, with a plastic daffodil pinned to the front. I took a stab in the dark and decided he was Welsh. I held out my hand, 'David Trick.' He extended his, 'Dai, Dai Watkins.' I was sitting next to the Welsh legend from the sixties and rugby league giant (5ft 6in) during the seventies. We spent a few minutes chatting about the likely outcome of the match. 'As long as the best team doesn't win we'll be okay,' he said. He, like everyone else, knew England had a great side and were red-hot favourites. I was so confident I remember saying, 'I'll eat this seat if we lose this one,' and I meant it. We were nailed on to proceed to the semi-finals.

As the teams left the pitch at half-time, things were not going well. Wales had scored two tries, luckily both unconverted, and England had managed a solitary Jonny Wilkinson penalty in reply. Even more worrying, Wales deserved to be in front. It genuinely felt as though England had stalled and were chasing shadows. My seat was close to the tunnel used by both teams and as Will Greenwood, the England centre, left the pitch a Welsh voice from nearby shouted out, 'Oi, Rodney, Rodney Trotter, not even Del Boy's going to get you out of this one.' Despite the desperate circumstances, I couldn't help but laugh. Not at the sentiment, but rather at how uncannily similar to Rodders Will Greenwood looked. England brought on Mike Catt in the second half and normal service was resumed, the England machine became more assured, and this coupled with a try by the aforementioned Mr Trotter, plus a further twenty points from the boot of Wilkinson, ensured an English victory 28–17 and an extended life for my seat and digestive system.

Following the match a group of us had decided to meet up in a Chinese restaurant. I knew we'd all reached middle age because earlier in the day we had made the decision to get something to eat post-match and reflect on the victory before launching ourselves into the stratosphere for a night of alcohol and song. We justified the decision by convincing ourselves all the drinking establishments would be full and the break for food would allow a few supporters to move on, leaving space for us in one of the many Brisbane bars. We'd need a seat after all.

There were ten of us in total and we were by no means muted. I like to think we were gathering our strength for the long night ahead. The conversation was dominated by the game we'd just seen and speculation about the semi-final against France in

Sydney the following week. We were halfway through the meal when a guy from another table approached ours. As soon as he opened his mouth it was clear he was an Aussie. 'Are you guys over here supporting England?' 'We are,' replied one of our party with a smug smile on his face.

He stared at us for a couple of seconds and said, 'If my team had won tonight, I'd be screaming and shouting, jumping and dancing and generally going nuts.'

To which one of the group, David Hill, a 6ft 4in policeman from the East End of London, replied, 'Which I think you'll find is why we sent you here just over two hundred years ago.'

The guys at our table along with a few others in earshot roared with laughter as our new Aussie mate raised his hands above his head in surrender and walked back to his seat in the corner of the restaurant.

One other incident I would like to share involves the accommodating nature of the reception-desk staff in Australian hotels. Our party had moved on to Sydney and as each day passed we got to know a little more about each other. One of the single guys, for the purpose of this story let's call him 'Log', was trying desperately to ingratiate himself with the local ladies. In fact, in the pursuit of veracity I'll remove the word 'local'. He was keen to get together with anything resembling the female form, ideally with a pulse. Night after night he struck out, though not through lack of effort or persistence on his part; he was a gold medallist in that department. In reality I think it might just have had something to do with him being several stone overweight, causing him to sweat profusely throughout the day and night.

We held the obligatory 'court session' for all tourists a couple of days before the semi-final. For those who have not toured and experienced a court session, there is an appointed judge, prosecution and defence counsel. All misdemeanours are brought to the attention of the judge by the prosecution. The judge then fines the individual concerned, forcing the miscreant to wear something ridiculous like a toilet seat around their neck for the next twenty-four hours, or perhaps to eat and drink everything the thirstiest and hungriest member of the court eats and drinks over a twelve-hour period. Just for your information, every charge is upheld, and the defence counsel is never utilised (apparently many years ago, someone asked to be represented by defence counsel who proceeded to do such a good job the defendant was found not guilty; the forfeit for being found not guilty was to be given twice the punishment).

I decided to produce some evidence for the judge to back up my claim that Log had persistently abandoned the boys in search of women and spent too much time in his hotel room watching films. To add spice to my accusation, I asked at reception if it were possible to put a few 'special films' onto a room bill and print it off, before deleting the extras from the record. 'No worries mate,' was the reply. 'What's the room number and how many do you want on there?'

'It's room 221 and could you put three on for me please.' He tapped a few keys on his keyboard, looked at me and said, 'There are four on there already, Sir.' Slightly shocked by the news, I asked if he could load an additional four movies onto the bill. Seconds later, the job was done and I entered the court room and quietly handed the incriminating evidence to the prosecution. Halfway through the court session Log was called to the bench.

The judge began in a suitable grave tone of voice, 'Mr Log, it has been brought to the attention of the court you have been spending more time annoying the opposite sex on this trip than you have with the boys, in addition to spending excessive time in your hotel room watching certain "films". We have all witnessed part of this charge first hand. Mr Prosecutor, do you have any evidence pertaining to the secondary charge?'

The room bill was produced and along with peanuts, Mars bars and water from the mini bar (who in their right mind ever gets anything out of their own mini bar?) the eight 'movies' were there for all to see.

Log immediately believed he'd been set up and scrutinised his bill closely, trying to work out what had happened. Eventually he had it. His defence.

'This is a fabricated bill, your honour. I know because I have only watched four "blueys" since we arrived and there are eight showing here.' It was pure Perry Mason.

Log was heavily punished: he was not allowed to communicate in any way with a member of the opposite sex for twenty-four hours, he also had to go for a shower every hour for twelve hours in order to cleanse his dirty body and mind, and for the duration of the court session he was ordered to stand in the corner, facing the room with his crown jewels in a bucket full of water and ice. The judge felt this would greatly assist in reducing his excessive libido.

Did it help? I don't know but I certainly never risked popping unannounced into his room to find out.

Taken for a Ride

Mark Regan

'Mark "Ronnie" Regan was born and bred in Bristol and is rightly proud of the city. He speaks "krek bristle", calling everyone "my bab" or "babber". Once you've worked out what he's saying you realise he's a passionate competitor who enjoyed imposing himself physically and verbally on opposition front rows. In the 2007 World Cup quarter-final against Australia, Andy Sheridan almost destroyed Aussie prop Matt Dunning in the first scrum, and as they broke up Ronnie was heard to say, "And you've got another seventy-nine minutes of f****** agony to look forward to, my babber."

'Ronnie's England breakthrough came when he succeeded Brian Moore in November 1995, for the

visit of world champions South Africa to Twickenham. He became the first player to make his England debut in the professional era of rugby union (incidentally I was the second Englishman to make his debut in the professional era when I came off the bench to win my first cap in the same game). He went on to gain forty-six caps, was a member of the successful 1997 British and Irish Lions tour to South Africa and played in the 2007 World Cup final.'

Everyone who follows rugby will remember England won the World Cup in 2003; those who follow the game a little more closely will also recall England won the Six Nations Grand Slam earlier in the same year.

In order to clinch the clean sweep England had to go over to Lansdowne Road in Dublin and defeat Ireland, no mean feat, particularly as Ireland had also remained undefeated in their previous four matches of the campaign and were hoping to win their first Grand Slam since 1948. Apart from a fantastic performance by England in securing a 42–6 victory, one of the most memorable moments from the day came just before kick-off. England came out of the tunnel and Martin Johnson lined us up in readiness for the national anthems on the left-hand side of the halfway line facing the stand we had just emerged from (the side normally reserved for the Irish team). Brian O'Driscoll, the Irish captain, did not appear overly perturbed about this but several of his players pointed out that England were standing in Ireland's rightful place and needed to move. One of the match-day co-ordinators was despatched to ask Johnno to shift his team about twenty metres to the right, but Captain Marvel was absolutely in the zone and had no intention of moving an inch, a fact he communicated in no uncertain terms to the poor bloke.

What made the situation extremely awkward for the hosts was that both teams were to be introduced to the Irish President Mary McAleese, and a forty-metre red carpet had been laid out either side of the halfway line. Ireland had three options: they could either stand in front of us (which would have been a great opportunity for each Englishman to have a word in the ear of the guy in front), they could stand to the right of us just behind the red carpet (where the visiting team would normally stand), or they could move to our left-hand side where there was no red carpet. They chose the third option with several of their team members standing on the far side of the twenty-two-metre line. From that moment we knew it was going to be our day. It was a brilliant piece of sports psychology by Johnno, upsetting practically everybody apart from the England team. We had an edge even before the whistle had blown to start the match.

Following the victory there was some celebrating to be done and another, not so public, memorable moment occurred. That night I found myself in a Dublin nightclub called Annabel's with my great mate, the England second-row forward Simon Shaw, who I should point out is not the 'fizziest drink in the fridge', is definitely 'a sandwich short of a full picnic' and without question is 'not the sharpest knife in the drawer'. We were standing at the bar listening to the music when Shawsie said to me, 'Richard Dunwoody has just arrived.' King Kong could have walked in and I wouldn't have been any the wiser. A height of 5ft 9in in a packed nightclub offers, at best, a view of a writhing mass of dancing bodies but no more. Shawsie's 6ft 8in gives him a distinct advantage over me when it comes to people spotting. 'Richard Dunwoody is my idol,' he went on to say. 'I've won so much money over the years backing him I'm going to go and say hello.' For those of you who don't follow horse racing, Richard Dunwoody is a three-time champion jump jockey and winner of the 1986 and 1994 Grand Nationals on West Tip and Miinnehoma respectively – a racing legend.

We walked over to Richard and introduced ourselves. Shawsie asked if he could buy the great man a drink and within a couple of minutes we were having a natter about the match. Well, when I say 'we' it was really just Richard and I. Shawsie was oddly distracted, which to be fair is not an unusual state to find him in, but when given the opportunity to chat with his idol I thought he might have been a touch more animated. He's probably desperate to steer the conversation away from rugby and on to horse racing, I concluded. Not unreasonable, I thought. How I wish I had been wrong.

Just as Mr Dunwoody and myself were beginning to struggle a bit to find further topics of interest, out of the blue Shawsie bailed me out in spectacular fashion. Looking down at his hero from his great height, he produced an immortal line that I will never, ever, forget. Nor, I suspect, will Richard Dunwoody.

'I would be honoured if you would ride me around the dance floor.'

Now, I'm not known as the most perceptive of fellows but

even I could tell this request had caught Dunwoody by surprise and was likely to receive a negative response. He looked up at Shawsie in amazement, 'Excuse me?'

Shawsie repeated, 'I would be honoured if you would ride me around the dance floor,' confirming what Dunwoody prayed he had misheard.

Thinking about it for less than a second Dunwoody simply replied, 'No.'

So 6ft 8in looks down at 5ft and a bit and says, 'You will ride me around the dance floor.' In defence of Simon Shaw, I think he'd had a beer or ten by this stage, and in defence of Richard Dunwoody, he probably recognised this fact and decided it was not the moment to deny the big man's request. So Shawsie got down on all fours and in something of a daze at the turn of events, I helped Dunwoody onto the big lump's back and off they went trotting around the dance floor. Needless to say, seconds later the whole place came to a standstill, the music was stopped, the main lights switched on and everyone tried to get a vantage point to watch the two sporting superstars cantering around the nightclub. After a couple of laps Dunwoody guided his mount back towards the bar where I helped him dismount. Shawsie then stood up and thanked Richard, who was understandably keen to move on before an even more bizarre request came his way. As we leaned against the bar, Shawsie turned to me and in a voice exuding genuine reverence, said, 'I can't believe that,' to which I replied, 'If I hadn't been here I wouldn't have believed it either. You've just had a champion jockey on your back riding you around a Dublin dance floor.'

'No, no, not that,' he said, as if I had just described an every-day event. 'I can't believe that when he slapped me on my arse with his beer bottle and squeezed his knees together, I actually felt as though I wanted to go a bit faster.'

If I had only suspected it before, that was the moment I *knew* it was time to make our way back to the hotel.

Pay Dirt

Frank Sheahan

'Frankie played for Munster on 154 occasions from 1996 to 2009 and was capped by Ireland twenty-nine times during a seven-year period ending in 2007 after the World Cup. As a hooker it was unfortunate for him that his first three years in the Irish squad were as understudy to the great Keith Wood. I have no doubt he would have gained many more caps had this not been the case.

'I have spent a few nights out with Frankie and am not in the least surprised his story has references to drinking and looking after team-mates who needed a drinking partner. Frankie founded Front Row, a company specialising in sponsorship and sports management, and has established an impressive client list, although it's interesting to

note The Crowne Plaza Melbourne is not amongst them. Read on.'

I was involved in two World Cups with the Irish team, 2003 and 2007, and my story comes from 2003 when I didn't play a game! I was what's commonly known as a 'dirt tracker'. For generations this title has been bestowed on members of a touring party who do not make the first team. On a regular tour the bigger matches take place on a Saturday and the dirt trackers play in the midweek games. A World Cup is different, however, with the management tending to field their best team, or as near as dammit, for every match as each one is critical. But even so, us dirt trackers are not just there for the ride, although I concede that this story may suggest otherwise. We also provide useful opposition to the primary team during training sessions. Honestly.

As I didn't make it onto the pitch for a single match in Australia, I selflessly assumed the role of unofficial captain of the trackers, a position I took very seriously. To my mind it was vital for squad harmony to ensure my fellow trackers were well occupied during the evenings when the main team was resting and focusing on the next match. Prior to our quarter-final against France in Melbourne my 'vice-captain', Anthony Horgan, was promoted to the bench so had to leave us behind, while at the same time Anthony Foley ('Axel') was dropped. As a Munster colleague and friend I took him under my wing and out for a couple of pints to ease the pain. I was only doing my duty. It was three days before the match, and Axel and I hooked up with former internationals Mick Galwey, John Langford and a couple of friends from back home. By 3.00 a.m. we were feeling no pain and my charge had forgotten all about losing his place in the team.

We were almost done for the night, when Axel decided he needed something to eat to round off his evening. The Crowne Plaza Hotel seemed the ideal solution as we knew it had a burger bar, which just happened to be situated on the same floor as the casino. I'd like to say we had a burger, but the reality is we had several in an effort to soak up the beer. So with stomachs full, batteries recharged and Axel only swaying slightly, we decided the night was still young. It was time to hit the poker tables. A dangerous decision given the vast quantities of alcohol we had consumed? Our fellow revellers certainly thought so, abandoning Axel and me in favour of a couple more drinks at the bar.

As we arrived at the table two people stood up to leave – so we took their seats and prepared for the first hand. The game was Caribbean Stud and I put down an opening bet of AUS$15. I also placed a AUS$1 bonus bet after it was explained to us that if I did so, provided I had at least a pair in my hand, I had a chance of winning the ever-increasing amount of money displayed in bright lights above the table. So with the cash down, the cards were dealt. I picked up my hand, looked at it and put it down immediately. I was more pissed than I realised. I couldn't have seen what I thought I had. Pull yourself together, Frank, there is serious money riding on this. I picked up the cards again and this time studied them more carefully, but the more I stared at them, the more confused I became. I was in a state, somewhere between high excitement and bewilderment. I put the cards down one last time, gave myself a moment and picked them up again. I wasn't hallucinating after all. I was definitely holding a Royal Flush, the best hand you can possibly be dealt.

Unlike normal poker, Caribbean Stud is played against the house (the dealer) and not the other players. If you win your hand you double your stake. I was set to pocket AUS$30, $15 of which was pure profit. Not too shabby for a minute or so's work. (There are other intricacies and forms of betting in the game but it's not necessary to go into these for the purposes of this story.) I was naturally excited and although you are not meant to, I couldn't resist sharing the moment with Axel. Leaning over I whispered to Foley, 'You're not going to believe what I have,' and was somewhat nonplussed when he replied, 'You're not going to believe what *I* have.' Still whispering I said, 'Seriously, you are not going to believe this hand.' He looked at me knowingly. 'Mate, I'm telling you, you are not going to f****** believe what I have.' Clearly this conversation was going nowhere so we waited for the dealer to turn over his last card. There are various rules about the house needing a certain minimum hand before the game can continue, and suffice to say the dealer did not have the required cards and the game folded. I was crushed. After all that, I would not be walking away AUS$15 to the good.

The other hands were turned over to reveal a pair, ace high, Axel's two pairs (not bad, but come on) before it came to me. Flipping my cards over, the dealer looked for a second and then in a very matter-of-fact fashion said, 'Royal Flush'. That's when it dawned on me. I still had my AUS$1 bonus bet running. When the realisation hit I started to jump around in celebration. It was hardly James Bond cool, but I didn't care. Then Axel grabbed me and reminded me it was the week of our match against France and perhaps we shouldn't be attracting any unnecessary attention. With some effort I sat down quietly as a small crowd gathered around the table including the floor manager, casino supervisor and the lads we'd been drinking with earlier. Cameras were checked to ensure everything was correct and above board and after about an hour it was confirmed I had won the jackpot, the amount displayed in neon lights above the table, AUS$93,633. I did spare a thought just then for the guy whose seat I had taken. He'd been one hand away from scooping the big prize. I felt sorry for him. But I got over it. Quickly.

I was given eighteen AUS$5,000 chips in addition to a few smaller denominations and made my way to the cashier's window. It must have looked like a scene from *Reservoir Dogs* as I stood there surrounded by several friends all in the 6ft-plus, 17st category. I could have taken the entire amount in a massive wad of notes but chose instead to accept a cheque for AUS$90,000 (which was deposited in my account when I returned home) and the rest in cash. Axel and I kept the win quiet as we didn't want the management to know we'd been out drinking and gambling in the small hours during the week of a match, but when we were eliminated from the tournament I came clean and everybody joined me in a celebratory drink or ten. I put my credit card behind the bar and told the lads to go for it. They didn't let me down. At the end of the evening I very happily settled a AUS$6,000 tab.

Would I have swapped my night out at the Plaza with being tucked up in bed, knowing I was going to be taking to the field in a few days to represent my country in the quarter-final of the World Cup? Let me think about that for a moment as I light this hand-rolled Cuban cigar with a 20 euro note . . .

Ain't Misbehavin'

Danny Grewcock

'A review of Danny's rugby career makes interesting reading, as this excerpt from the website borntoruck.com highlights:

> During this time, he managed to amass 69 England caps, 4 Lions caps, a World Cup winner's medal together with 226 appearances in the blue, black and white of Bath. But Danny Grewcock will always be somewhat fondly remembered as a fantastic accumulator of suspensions. We can't quite decide which was our favourite; the 2 week ban for clouting Lawrence Dallaglio in the 2003 Parker Pen final [not my personal favourite, by the way] or the 6 weeks for clobbering Clermont's Thibault

Privat in the 2007 Challenge Cup final. Actually, it might just be the 2 months for biting Kevin Mealamu's finger which inexplicably found its way into his mouth during the 1st Lions v All Blacks Test in 2005.

'For anyone who has ever met Danny the words above will appear incongruous to say the least. He is one of the best guys around, always willing to have a word with supporters and a great friend to the community department at Bath who consistently called on his services throughout his career. To add some balance I should point out he played in all three Test matches for the Lions against Australia in 2001 and in six of the ten provincial matches. The tour brought out the best in Danny as he matched the performances of fellow lock Martin Johnson with some of the best rugby of his career.

'After the 2003 World Cup he returned to domestic rugby union with Bath and produced some outstanding rugby, which led to his international recall as the successor to Johnno in the Six Nations. He was arguably England's player of the tournament, while his club form remained superb.

'Huge thanks to both Danny Grewcocks for their contribution to this book.'

Although I managed to play sixty-nine times for England I always seemed to miss out on the big occasions. My international career could not have started better, scoring a try on my debut while touring Argentina with England in 1997, but from that moment on referees played an inordinately large part in my progress (or lack of it). I feel I was often misunderstood in my playing days. I was never the aggressor in any situation. It was just that I was often standing close to an injustice and merely sought to save the referee time and effort by exacting swift retribution and restoring the natural balance.

However, having been selected to represent England in the 2003 World Cup I was determined to make the most of the opportunity. I knew I'd been lucky to gain selection to the squad and was under no illusions that with Martin Johnson, the best second row in the world in my eyes, and Ben Kay (not far behind), it was going to be difficult to break up the partnership. Even so, I was going to push them as hard as I could, which meant, in addition to putting maximum effort into every training session and every match, I was going to follow all the instructions issued by Clive Woodward and his team. To the letter.

Clive spent years preparing for the tournament. He'd assembled the best coaches to support the physical activity as well as an array of backroom staff, all experts in their relative fields. The phrase 'leaving no stone unturned' was often used in media reports and to be honest they were accurate. Clive was constantly in search of anything that would give his team a slight edge in any area related to the game. I couldn't imagine how it was possible for England to gain 'an edge' on the opposition during the flight from England to Perth three weeks prior to the start of the tournament, but Clive, being a much deeper and more lateral thinker than me (not really much of a compliment that, sorry Clive), was on the case.

He didn't want his squad of players disrupted by the different time zones and consequent jetlag we were bound to suffer when arriving on the other side of the world, so he'd been in consultation with one of his team of experts and devised an in-flight programme which would negate such problems. We were each given a full schedule of things we needed to do. For instance, at a specific time a member of the medical team would give everyone a vitamin pill and a quantity of water, and we would then be told to walk up and down the aisles for ten minutes before being ordered to sleep for a period of time. No matter how deep the sleep, at the appointed hour we were woken in order to take another vitamin pill, and so it continued throughout the flight. However, while I can't fault the philosophy, I was acutely aware that every time I was ordered to go to sleep I had the energy of a spring lamb and when woken felt like a bear halfway through hibernation.

We arrived in Perth and I felt like shit. All I wanted to do was go to bed and get some rest. However, the schedule stated we needed to resist the desire to sleep and battle on until 10.30 p.m. when we could crash out. The theory being we would wake the following morning feeling on top of the world and fully in tune with the time zone. With my new philosophy in place, I was prepared to follow the schedule in its entirety. I wandered around Perth, drinking several cups of strong espresso, I explored the hotel, occasionally going into my room to look longingly at the bed, until finally 10.30 p.m. arrived and I collapsed into it.

As had been predicted, come morning I awoke refreshed and

ready to face the challenges of the day. I filled the kettle to make a cup of coffee and while waiting for it to boil I noticed how effective the blackout curtains were in my room. I wandered over and pulled them apart making sure my eyes were almost shut to protect them from the shocking brightness of the sun's glare. I needn't have bothered. With the curtains wide apart there was no noticeable increase in the light filtering into my room. A glance at my watch told me it was 1.00 a.m. I'd never felt as alive as I did at that moment. I sent a couple of texts to friends and family back in England, I even contemplated using the one sheet of stationery on the bureau and writing a letter, something I'd not done since schooldays. By 3.00 a.m. I was prowling the corridors making my way to the breakfast room which on arrival I noticed opened at 6.00 a.m.

After an hour or so I returned to my room thinking I must be the only person suffering as I hadn't seen another member of the England party during my nocturnal travels. Eventually at 5.30 a.m. I returned to the breakfast room in the hope it would open early; although there was no food available a waiter did bring me a cup of coffee, which was much appreciated as for the first time in nearly five hours I was beginning to feel a bit drowsy. At 6.10 a.m. the first member of the England party appeared at the entrance and it didn't take a genius to work out from his look that he'd been suffering as I had. His eyes were bloodshot and he was obviously a little disorientated as he bumped into a table on his way to the hot buffet. Patriotic as ever, he filled his plate with a Full English and made his way towards where I was sitting. With each step I began to reassess my initial diagnosis. I could see he was having a bit of a struggle walking while carrying his fully laden plate at the same time. Within seconds of sitting down opposite me two things became apparent. Firstly, he was not suffering from jetlag, secondly he was 'arseholed', his bloodshot eyes merely a by-product of a massive night on the piss.

The man in question was, of course, the great Jason Leonard OBE, who went on to explain how he didn't subscribe to 'fancy dan' schedules. His tried and trusted method of overcoming jetlag was to get 'straight on it' and meet the locals (which apparently he did from the moment we landed twenty-hours previously). Jason went on to feature largely in the World Cup, while I missed the initial games with a toe injury and didn't make my first appearance until the match against the mighty Uruguay, where I broke my hand and took no further part in the competition.

Four years later and I was hopeful of making the 2007 World Cup squad, I'd had a reasonable season with Bath and a few rugby journalists were tipping me for selection. As it happened my name didn't even appear on the list for consideration. Yet another referee had misunderstood my actions during a match and I was the subject of a suspension, the timing of which coincided perfectly with the tournament dates.

Old Men of the Sea

Martin Corry

'Martin is yet another former England captain making a contribution to this book. "Cozza" played for Tunbridge Wells, Newcastle Gosforth and Bristol in his early career before joining Leicester Tigers, where he remained for thirteen seasons until his retirement from the sport in 2009. He gained sixty-four caps for England and also played for the British and Irish Lions in 2001 and 2005.

'He was a versatile player who played at No. 8, blindside and in the second row. Such flexibility normally leads to individuals being selected to sit on the bench as they can cover so many positions. It's testament to Martin's ability that he rarely occupied a place as replacement, forcing selectors to pick him for the starting fifteen.

'Proving rugby union is a compassionate sport, Martin was allowed to fly home during the 2003 World Cup to attend the birth of his first child, a daughter called Eve, before rejoining the squad a few days later. His son Edward was born (more conveniently) after the Six Nations Championship in 2006.

'Martin was called up as a replacement to the Lions tour of Australia in 2001, primarily due to the injury of one of the key members of the squad. Well, me at any rate. He impressed the coach Graham Henry from the moment he arrived and played in all three Tests. Even though he was replacing me, I have to say in my opinion he was possibly the player of the tour and thoroughly deserved his place in the team.'

Many things have been written about Sir Clive Woodward, particularly since England's victory in the 2003 World Cup. Overwhelmingly the copy has been positive and quite rightly so; he was the architect of our success, responsible for putting all the pieces of the jigsaw together. He ensured we had the best facilities, the best coaches, in short everything he could think of to prepare team fully for the challenge ahead.

However in order to get everything right, it goes without saying mistakes will have been made, which is no bad thing.

Without them it is almost impossible to learn. I believe one such error occurred during a trip to Australia involving an intensive course of strength and conditioning prior to the 1999 World Cup. The main objective was to increase bulk and body mass and therefore entailed a huge amount of incredibly tough weight training. As we had all come to expect, everything had been planned well in advance with individual programmes designed for every member of the squad and targets set for increased strength and weight.

As an illustration of the intensity of the programme Clive and his team had devised, one exercise stands out. I put my heart and soul into this exercise in an attempt to impress both my team-mates and Clive. The instruction given was to bench press a set weight, let's say 120kg for me, until it became impossible to manage one more repetition. Twenty kilos were then removed from the bar and the exercise continued until once again the point of no return was reached, whereupon a further 10kg was removed from each end. By the end I was left with the 20kg bar alone, which after about half a dozen very dodgy lifts seemed to take on the form of an elephant carrying a house. I couldn't have lifted a feather, let alone this instrument of torture which was now pinning me down to my bench. I was surely done for, unable to move and barely breathe, until my training partner Lawrence Dallaglio came to my rescue. If he hadn't removed the bar from across my chest I think I'd have remained there for ever. I had absolutely no strength left; a five year old girl would have beaten me in an arm wrestle.

Regardless of the pain we endured every day on that trip, there was one significant plus – the joy us forwards took in 'occasionally' taking the piss out of the backs as they struggled to lift what appeared to us to be nothing more than drinking straws with a couple of Polo mints stuck on each end. Such mockery of our team-mates, however, was only ever going to come back and haunt us and sure enough a few weeks later Clive organised a speed and conditioning course which inevitably featured the backs skipping past us on a regular basis, smiling as they changed from third to fourth gear. We only went up to second. I was briefly nicknamed 'Tank' during this period, not, I am afraid to say, because of my fearsome power and explosive weaponry on the pitch, but rather because every time I put my foot on the internal accelerator there was no noticeable change of pace. Hard to argue against. It was a clear indication that it takes all sorts to build a successful team.

But back to the strength and body mass programme in Australia. After days of intensive sweat and grunting Clive had organised a treat for the squad, a day of deep sea fishing. With the benefit of hindsight, I think a night in a bar would have been a better, and safer, option. After all, he would hardly have been risking any great alcohol-induced disaster, not one of us had the strength to lift even a pint. A couple of gin and tonics drunk through a straw would have probably been our limit before we crawled off to bed. However, fishing it was, which I have to say I wasn't overly keen on, knowing that although my mind's eye saw a blue marlin writhing at the end of my line, my body screamed for nothing larger than a small mackerel. Still, in the interest of team spirit I agreed to participate in Clive's day of rest and recuperation.

As we boarded the boat, the sea was calm and spirits were lifting. The banter between the players was returning and I began to look forward to a day of drifting around the ocean dropping my line in the hope of wrestling that mackerel onto the deck. An hour out to sea and the boat began to rock, twenty minutes later and we were no more than a cork tossed around by the huge swell. The boys were falling like flies as sea sickness engulfed the squad. For those who have never experienced such dreadful nausea, I can remember two distinct phases. The first is when you think you are going to die, followed by the sad realisation you are not.

I went in search of the team doctor, Terry Crystal, who would doubtless have some pills and potions to speed my recovery. I found Terry below deck. He was the strangest shade of grey/green I'd ever seen. Simon Le Bon in the *Rio* video he most certainly was not.

'Terry do you have any sickness tablets?' I shouted.

'They don't bloody work,' he replied. 'I've taken six already.'

Several hours later we returned to port and if memory serves me well there were only two members of the party unaffected by the elements: Clive Woodward and our defence coach Phil Larder. The rest of us had emptied the entire contents of our stomachs onto the boat and into the ocean, and continued to dry heave for many hours to come.

After a week or so of building strength and body mass, the majority of the squad looked almost skeletal twenty-four hours after our 'treat'. It was not Clive's finest moment, but one he learnt from. Those blue marlins could swim the ocean safe in the knowledge that no English rugby player was going to come anywhere near them again, as long Clive remained in charge. I'm sure the intensive training did some good but to a man we were all lighter, felt weaker and looked ten years older when we returned home to continue our preparations for the 1999 World Cup.

Official Respect

Matt Dawson

'Matt needs little introduction, although I know if I didn't give him a decent one he'd do it himself. Perhaps one thing about Matt that not many people know is that he's a member of a select group of two people: English players who have two World Cup winner's medals, one from the inaugural World Cup Rugby Sevens tournament in Scotland in 1993 and the other from the 2003 tournament in Australia. I know you now want to know the identity of the other member of this group ... modesty prevents me ... okay, it's me, and I'm sure Matt is as proud of this achievement as I am.

'Matt gained seventy-seven caps for England and completed a grand slam of British and Irish Lions tours to South Africa, Australia and New

Zealand, playing in seven Tests. As a player he had many assets, not least his vision from the base of a scrum and his ability to grab the ball when awarded a penalty and create mayhem and confusion in the opposition defence. Few will forget the superb try he scored in the first Lions Test against South Africa in 1997 when he broke from a scrum and threw a simply outrageous dummy that "checked" four Springbok defenders, leaving the try line at his mercy.

'Since retirement from rugby, while trying to keep his light under a bushel, he has continued to demonstrate his many talents. He is a former winner of BBC's *Celebrity Master Chef*, came a very close second to cricketer Mark Ramprakash in *Strictly Come Dancing* and is a team captain on the ever-popular *Question of Sport*. He also finds time to present his own programme on BBC Radio 5 Live and appears on various TV food programmes. My spies tell me he recently featured in an edition of a www.888.com TV poker special where he ended up winning second prize, which in itself is a great achievement, but knowing Matt as I do, I have no doubt he will be entering again in order to claim the big pot.

'And needless to say, Matt wasn't content to just pass on the one story as requested. No, that's not

Matt's style. He had to give me two. "They were both too good to drop one." Don't you just love him?'

In Need of Modernisation

The date 22 November 2003 is etched into my memory for all time, the day England beat Australia in the World Cup final at the Telstra Stadium, Sydney. A story often told at dinners by various members of the team involves the South African referee on that famous evening, Andre Watson.

Even at club level, referees tend to visit both changing rooms in order to give players a few pointers on how they intend to officiate the match, and information gleaned from these informal chats can often be useful during the game. You get a feel for what the ref is going to be very hot on, and conversely what he is likely to let go. A World Cup final is no different.

Andre arrived in the England changing room and talked generally to the entire team; for some reason he felt it his duty to remind us what a big game lay ahead. As if after months (in fact years) of preparation we were likely to have forgotten what was at stake. He then spoke specifically to the forwards, and as scrum-half I felt I needed to hear what he had to say. In his harsh Dutch Afrikaans accent he explained that in his opinion the scrum was likely to play a big part in the game, so he would not be awarding any penalties unless he was absolutely certain which side or individual caused the offence. In fact he went on to say, 'I will need to be so certain, confident enough to "stake my mortgage" on making the correct decision.' Our eight forwards all seemed pleased with the news. I looked at our front-row men Phil Vickery, Steve Thompson and Trevor Woodman and tried to imagine their thoughts. Perhaps they went something like, 'If we do nothing illegal during the scrums then we have nothing to worry about.' Get a grip Dawson. Much more likely they are along the lines of, 'As long as we are reasonably subtle we'll be able to try a few tricks.' No, that still wasn't right. They would never come up with the word 'subtle'. Then I had it: 'If we don't do anything too thick we'll get away with bloody murder!' Andre then turned to me to say a few words. Normally this would be along the lines of, 'Make sure you put the ball in straight at scrums,' or a directive regarding his policy on taking quick tap penalties. On this occasion, however, he got straight to the point. 'You, Dawse, don't be a twat today.'

Twenty minutes later we listened to a last few words from Martin Johnson and left the safety of the changing room for the pitch. Anyone reading this who attended the final could have been forgiven for thinking they'd arrived at a weird music concert instead of the World Cup. Kick-off was preceded by performances including Kate Ceberano singing 'True Colours' (a theme throughout the tournament) and the Sydney's Children Choir and the Rugby World Choir giving us a rendition of the official theme song, 'World in Union'. Following these performances, the traditional national anthems were performed and finally we could get on with the business of playing the most important rugby match of our lives.

Everyone remembers Jonny's winning dropped goal late into the second period of extra-time, but people often forget just how close we were to winning the match in normal time. Sixty-one minutes into the game Elton Flatley was successful with a penalty kick taking the score to 14–11 in England's favour. It was not until the eightieth minute of the match he converted another penalty to tie the scores at 14–14. The penalty was awarded following a scrum! As both packs made contact, Andre Watson blew his whistle and said, 'Incorrect engagement, penalty Australia.' All the English forwards stared at him in disbelief, Lawrence Dallaglio's chin dropped as that 'what the f*** are you talking about' look appeared on his face. However, the decision was made and unlike modern-day footballers, it was accepted and everyone retreated the obligatory ten metres. As we made our way back to face the penalty, our hooker Steve Thompson was clearly thinking over all he had heard from Andre in the changing room, about having to be absolutely certain of a scrum offence before awarding a penalty and being prepared to stake his mortgage on being correct. The one thing England would not have done in the last minute of the World Cup final was deliberately give a penalty away. With all these thoughts running around his head Tommo turned to the referee and said, 'Andre, you must have a shit house.'

What the Bleep is Happening?

Other players have no doubt contributed stories about the celebrations that followed our victory over Australia, and believe me they were massive; my own recollection centres on our departure from Sydney for the flight home to England. Incidentally, when we arrived at Heathrow we had no idea so many people were going to make the effort to come to the airport and welcome us back. In some respects rugby union is the poor relation to football in the UK and understandably so; however, all of us were treated to a small glimpse into the worlds of Premier League players and film stars when we entered the arrivals lounge and were met by a barrage of faces and flashing cameras.

Back to Sydney, where even though we felt special, we were treated exactly the same as everyone else. We had to go through the usual procedures of checking in, getting our bags weighed, collecting our boarding passes and going through security. It was at that final stage where my incident occurred. I was waiting in line along with the rest of the squad and to be honest not really paying too much attention to the notices and verbal requests urging all passengers to remove their loose change and belts etc. When it was my turn to walk through the metal detector I strolled up to the arch and wondered, as we all do, if it would go off or let me through unhindered. Two loud bleeps gave me my answer. There followed the expected hilarious quips from the boys behind me, such as 'It's probably his metal hip', 'Take him away and do an internal inspection' and other timeless classics. As the barrage of smart-ass comments continued I realised I had not removed my watch so I walked back through the detector, took off the watch and placed it in one of the plastic tubs and sent it on its way to the scanner. I then confidently walked through the archway for my second attempt only to be once again greeted with the high-pitched electric alert.

The security guy who had to deal with me was obviously coming towards the end of a long shift and had decided nothing was going to make him smile, in particular a cocky English scrum-half who was part of the team that had pinched the trophy I am sure he felt rightly belonged to Australia. I apologised as I took out a handful of change from my pocket, walked back once more and deposited the offending coins in another plastic tub. Feeling certain I was home and dry for sure now I marched through for the third time only to once again hear that familiar sound.

Mister Airport Security had obviously had enough and pointed towards the two yellow feet on the floor indicating I should place my own feet on them so he could search me with his wand. He waved it silently up and down my left then right leg and around my midriff. I was beginning to wonder if the dental work I'd received over the years contained enough metal to set off a sensitive airport machine. The guard continued his wand waving along each of my arms and as it passed my chest something triggered a loud buzzing. A smile appeared on my face as I realised what had been detected. The guard stiffened, took one pace back and asked me to unbutton my shirt. With hindsight he was probably under the impression I had a knife taped to my chest and wanted to be a safe distance away in case I became a threat. I undid two buttons and slowly reached inside my shirt. I could tell the guard was now on 'full alert' as I grabbed the offending article and held it a few inches away from my body for him to inspect.

'I'm sorry, mate,' I said as I dangled my World Cup winner's medal in front of his face, 'but now it's out, you may as well take a good look because it's going to be at least four years and probably longer before you see one of these again.'

Did he see the funny side of it? No, he didn't, but fair play to him he had probably been on the wrong end of jubilant English fans taking the mickey for hours. He briefly questioned my parentage before allowing me to collect my belongings from the various receptacles which were by now clogging up the security scanner.

The Thousandth Time

Ben Kay

'Ben and I have become inextricably linked as a result of pub quizzes around the country:

Q1. Who was the only member of the squad to play every minute of every game in England's successful 2003 World Cup campaign?
A. Lawrence Dallaglio
Q2. Which England player repeated the achievement during the 2007 World Cup campaign when England lost the final to South Africa?
A. Ben Kay

'Ben is also one of only four players to be in the starting line-up for England at both World Cup finals, the other three being Jonny Wilkinson, Jason Robinson and Phil Vickery.

'Ben played sixty-two Test matches for England scoring two tries along the way (should have been three, sorry for mentioning it, Ben). He made his England debut against Canada on 2 June 2001, displacing Danny Grewcock from the England side (there's a reasonable chance Danny may have been suspended at the time). He also played nearly 300 games for Leicester Tigers during his eleven seasons with the club.

'Ben was one of the most highly rated middle line-out jumpers in world rugby. Add this to his surprising athleticism for a man weighing around 18st (115kg) and standing 6ft 6in, and you end up with a formidable second-row forward, someone I was always pleased to have on my side when playing for England.

'Since retirement from the game at the end of the 2009–10 season he has become a popular commentator for the ESPN channel during their coverage of the Aviva Premiership.'

The England victory in the World Cup final 2003 has been covered extensively by radio, television and the written media. Every highlight and every mistake has been scrutinised, analysed and talked to death, in my opinion anyway. I suppose if my name was Jonny Wilkinson I wouldn't feel this way, but in these circumstances unfortunately I'm Ben Kay and when it comes to the World Cup final there's only one thing people want to talk about. If only I had a pound for every time I've been asked, 'How did you drop that ball with the line at your mercy?'

It was about half an hour into the game and I was wide on the right-hand side of the field where the winger would normally stand. Was I there by chance or was I such a great reader of the game I knew the ball was going to end up where I'd positioned myself? The truth is I was knackered and decided to have a short rest away from the action, but before I had a chance to catch my breath, the action decided to come to me. The ball was whipped along the line and Matt Dawson, our scrum-half, passed me a ball which I would have caught nine hundred and ninety-nine times out of a thousand. Unfortunately it happened to be the thousandth time and it spilled out of my hands with the try line just inches away. The answer is, I don't know how I dropped it, I just did.

Things would have been worse for me had we not gone on to win the match (thank you, Jonny). I would have probably been haunted by that one moment for the rest of my life. As it is, we are now eight years on and occasionally a couple of days do go by without anyone mentioning it, so it's not too bad.

Although I made the mistake, I put it to one side after the game and concentrated on the fact I was a member of a World Cup-winning team. I did in fact play in every England match apart from the one against Uruguay, so felt I had made a decent contribution along the way. I celebrated long into the night with the rest of the boys and most of the next day too.

We had been a confident side – not arrogant – and we all believed we were capable of winning the tournament, so when the victory came it was a moment of pure elation, the culmination of a lot of hard work. It was not necessarily a surprise; the surprise for me was the unbelievable scenes at Heathrow when we arrived home in the early hours of the morning. Literally thousands of people had made the effort to get to the airport at some ungodly time to show their appreciation of the achievement. This was then eclipsed by the reported half a million people who lined the streets up to thirty deep when we made the open-top bus tour from Marble Arch to Trafalgar Square with the Webb Ellis Cup. From the top of the bus wherever I looked the scenes were simply breathtaking. People were hanging out of office windows, standing on top of buildings, many waving flags and displaying homemade banners.

It was during this bus tour that it became clear to me that the World Cup was officially over. Not because of the obvious – we were displaying the cup – it was more subtle than that. Clive Woodward (soon to become a knight of the realm) had looked after every detail of the campaign; he was clearly not responsible for ordering the open-top bus. I knew this from the moment I realised it didn't have a toilet. With the celebrating we had done before the journey it was not so much a luxury as a priority. Things were desperate; I have seen some photographs taken that day and to be honest there's many a grimace on the faces of certain players which could be mistaken for smiles. The reality was they were crossing their legs and fighting an almost uncontrollable urge to urinate. Most managed to control themselves. Some didn't. Jason Leonard was seen using an empty champagne bottle as a receptacle, a feat which required considerable coordination, far more than Jason was capable of. He blames it on the bus making a sudden stop. From the death-defying velocity of ... three miles an hour. But it was enough to put Jason off balance, causing some of the contents of the bottle and the remainder of what he had inside him to go over the trouser leg of Lewis Moody. Jason was feeling no pain and was probably not even aware of the accident while Lewis continued waving at the crowds seemingly oblivious to the large damp patch on his right leg.

Following the bus trip we went to Buckingham Palace to meet the Queen, a huge honour for us all. Before being presented we were briefed on etiquette.

'Stand when the Queen enters the room. While it is not expected of you to bow, you may if you like. A man could bow his head from his neck. If Her Majesty extends her gloved hand to you, simply touch it briefly. A firm handshake would be discouraged.

'Address the Queen as "Your Majesty". Thereafter, each time you speak you would use "Ma'am". If you address others in the royal family, male or female, the initial greeting would be "Your Royal Highness" followed by "Sir" or "Ma'am."

'Pick appropriate topics of conversation. Don't discuss private issues or something you've read in the tabloids.'

Fully prepared, we awaited her arrival. After a few minutes inside the Palace, and some nervous chat amongst the players, the doors opened and in walked the Queen preceded by several corgis, all of whom made a bee-line for Lewis's trouser leg much to his surprise and embarrassment. The Queen remained with us for about twenty minutes and had her photograph taken with the squad (it's interesting to note the two corgis in the photo, one either side of Lewis seated in the front row).

Our captain Martin Johnson introduced each of us individually to the Queen. As she worked her way down the line towards me I wondered what I should say to her. Having not read the tabloid press for several weeks I was relaxed about the possibility of making a *faux pas*. Martin extended his arm in my direction and said, 'This is my partner in the second row, Ben Kay.' The Queen extended her hand, which I touched lightly, looked up at me and said, 'So tell me, Ben, how did you manage to drop that ball with the line at your mercy?'

2007

The staging of the 2007 Rugby World Cup returned to the northern hemisphere as France took its turn to welcome rugby's most prestigious event. Once again a small number of matches were due to be played away from the host country, this time in Cardiff's Millennium Stadium and Edinburgh's Murrayfield. England had become the first nation from outside the southern hemisphere to win the trophy four years earlier and the French supporters fully expected France to become the second. The weight of expectation on 'Les Bleus' was enormous.

Once again there were twenty teams participating. The eight automatic qualifiers were the quarter-finalists from 2003, leaving this time eighty-six countries competing for the remaining twelve places. The structure of the tournament remained the same with four pools of five teams, the top two qualifying for the knockout rounds.

South Africa shared the same pool as England and stuffed us 36–0, the one and only time England have failed to score in a World Cup match. The defeat was a massive blow to England, although on a personal note I thought I made a decent contribution (I was dropped from the side after our match against the USA and was left bellowing from the stand, which I did very well). While this was a dismally one-sided affair, a number of other pool matches provided far greater entertainment value, most notably the contest between Fiji and Wales, one of the best ever seen.

Wales arrived in Nantes for their do-or-die clash with the Fijians knowing defeat would see them crash out at the pool stage for a third time in World Cup history. The match was rated as the best pool game of the entire tournament by the IRB official tournament website, www.rugbyworldcup.com, and proved to be one of the most enthralling seesaw battles in international rugby (perhaps not for Welsh supporters).

Wales took an early lead at the Stade de la Beaujoire courtesy of a Stephen Jones penalty goal. However Welsh fans were in for a rough ride as they witnessed their team concede three tries in the space of a whirlwind ten minutes. At 25–3 Wales were staring down a barrel but they rallied after this devastating opening period dominated by Fijian flair and power. Alix Popham's try on thirty-four minutes reduced the deficit and James Hook's conversion left Wales trailing at half-time by fifteen points. Wales restarted with more purpose and were aided with the sin-binning, on the stroke of half-time, of Fijian try-scorer Qera after he kneed a Welsh player. The extra-man advantage allowed Wales to creep steadily back into the game. Shane Williams notched a try five minutes in, his sixth of the tournament, and Jones's conversion took Wales to within a converted score of the opposition. Gareth Thomas duly provided the much-needed try, marking his century of appearances in a Welsh shirt, but the conversion went astray to keep Fiji ahead by just two points. The lead then changed hands several times before a try five minutes from the end of the match by prop Graham Dewes secured a victory for Fiji 38–34. Wales were on their way home prematurely once again.

France lost unexpectedly to Argentina in their opening pool match but still finished second in the group, which meant a quarter-final against the much-fancied All Blacks (when aren't they much fancied?). Similar to their encounter in 1999, the French overturned a first-half deficit, winning 20–18, leaving their entire nation anticipating a first World Cup final victory. Unfortunately they needed to win their semi-final first. Sadly for the French, England spoilt the party with a 14–9 win which took us to our third final, and left the hosts to lament what might have been.

South Africa, who'd walloped England a few weeks earlier, provided the opposition. By half-time we were 9–3 down but still in the match. A few minutes after the break, Mark Cueto appeared to wriggle over the try line following a brilliant solo run from English centre Matthew Tait. After almost ten minutes of analysis the video ref decided Cueto's foot was on the touchline as he grounded the ball. No try. We lost the match 15–6 and the disappointment was palpable. Even though we'd started the tournament badly and in some respects limped into the final, it didn't change the gut-wrenching feeling of defeat. It was a particularly sad moment for me as I knew my involvement in Rugby World Cups as a player was over. But what a ride I'd had.

On the plus side I'll be out in New Zealand later this year, cheering England with no worries about training sessions and personal fitness. I can join the ranks of supporters and find out what I've been missing all these years. I look forward to seeing you there.

Text Book Selection Process

This tournament was always going to be a different experience for me from the one in 2003, for a number of reasons. Firstly, it was going to be my last World Cup. After twelve years of international rugby combined with seventeen years of club rugby with Wasps I knew my body was not going to hold out for too much longer (certainly not another four years). Secondly, in 2003 the squad was very settled and full of confidence going into the tournament, on the back of a Six Nations Grand Slam and a world ranking of No. 1. Four years on and the squad had not enjoyed the stability of 2003, finishing third in the Six Nations, losing by eight points to Wales and heavily to Ireland, and with a world ranking of No. 7, one place below Argentina.

Looking back I think our coach Brian Ashton had originally pencilled me in as one of the starting XV but for whatever reason, he changed his mind as the tournament progressed. I did, however, start one match, our opener against the USA, who frustrated us for long periods of time and in all honesty I played like a drain, getting sin-binned towards the end. Now that I think about it, perhaps that had something to do with Brian's decision. Anyway, as I mentioned earlier I was then dropped for the next match, the 36–0 drubbing we endured against South Africa, which I watched from the stand. You may notice I say 'we endured' because even though I was not on the pitch it was still a result the whole squad felt responsible for.

That said, I'd be lying if I didn't admit to thinking that the manner of our defeat might just open the door to my recall. I was still ambitious and genuinely convinced I had something to offer the team. And in fact I was recalled, eventually, to the bench for the final group game against Tonga. But at least that gave me the possibility of coming on at some point, which I did in the sixty-fourth minute. From there on, that was the level of my involvement, a sixty-something-minute replacement in all the subsequent games, up to and including the final.

I think of myself as a professional and during the team's training sessions, even with my eighty-plus caps, I was honestly more than happy to hold the tackling bag so a guy with five caps could knock it over. There was only one moment I can remember when the situation got to me and a fleeting thought shot across my mind as one of the newer boys smashed into me and hit the deck. 'While you're down there you couldn't tie my bootlaces could you, mate?' As I say, it was only momentary and I caught myself. 'For f**** sake, Lawrence, stop it. No he f****** well can't.' I wasn't bitter. Honestly. I just thought it would be more advantageous to have me on the field of play rather than twiddling my thumbs and eating sweets on the bench. Unfortunately the decision was out of my hands.

During the pool phase of the tournament we'd been staying in a beautiful hotel near the Chateau de Versailles, but having progressed to the quarter-finals the show moved to Marseille. My previous visit to the city had been with England during the reign of Clive Woodward and on that occasion our accommodation had been the Hotel Sofitel Marseille, Vieux Port, known as 'the best address in Marseille'. Imagine my delight then when in 2007 we checked into the Holiday Inn. There were three other teams staying in Marseille at the time, South Africa, Fiji and Australia, and apparently lots had been drawn to determine the allocation of hotels. The South African team drew the Hotel Sofitel, and I can only assume we finished fourth.

On entering my room I was instantly engulfed by an incredible, awful smell. I had never in my life (and haven't since) endured such a pungent aroma and as I made my way towards the window in a desperate bid for fresh air it occurred to me there must be a decomposing body hidden in the wardrobe. No such luck. Through stinging eyes I saw the source of the problem. Someone, or something, had been sick over the bedspread, carpet and bedside chair. Horrendous.

It transpired the Georgian rugby team, beaten by France the previous day, had also drawn the short straw and been staying in our hotel. Clearly the player who had occupied my room had either been celebrating their one and only victory in the pool stages, over Namibia a week earlier, or had possibly scored Georgia's try in the 64–7 defeat against the hosts. Either way, things had clearly got out of control and the dear chap had ended up emptying the contents of his stomach all over my hotel room. The maid had presumably entered the room, sniffed the air, glimpsed the various piles of sick and, with a Gallic shrug of the shoulders, turned on her heels and departed for the next room on her list.

I remained calm as I described the state of my room to the receptionist and asked if I could possibly be moved. Surprise surprise, there was a Rugby World Cup on and the hotel was fully booked. I was asked to vacate the room for a couple of hours while the cleaners took care of the situation. I can absolutely guarantee if I walked into that room today the smell would still be there. Two hours of cleaning and a Shake 'n' Vac was not going to put the freshness back.

I left the hotel and walked across the road to a small espresso bar, sipping strong coffee and contemplating how the mighty had fallen. Four years ago I had been in the Telstra Stadium, Sydney, with a World Cup winner's medal around my neck, and now I'd been relegated to the bench and asked to sleep in a vomit-filled room. I needed to take control.

Feeling utterly miserable as I stared through the window of the café I noticed a Eurocar hire centre next to the hotel. A plan began to formulate. I walked over and asked for the best car they had available. Moments later, with the paperwork completed and my credit card laden with more debt, it was time for part two of operation 'Cheer up Lawrence'. I sent a text to my fellow bench members asking them to meet me in reception in ten minutes. While I waited for the boys I phoned the restaurant Cinquante Cinq in St Tropez and booked a table for six of us. Club 55 was well known as a destination for the better-behaved and less boisterous element of the St Tropez crowd. I fully intended to put a small dent in that reputation.

The lads arrived as requested and I explained we were going on a little trip to the beach, and they needn't bother packing their trunks. The squad had the day off and after a couple of questions everyone was up for the adventure. I called Dan Luger (a former England team-mate), who was playing his rugby in Nice at the time, and told him we would pick him up on the way. Within two hours we are all at Cinquante Cinq, seated at an outside table with our feet in the sand overlooking the Mediterranean Sea, sipping chilled rosé. Life was beginning to feel much better.

At this point I had no idea that during the car journey scrum-half Pete Richards's phone had slipped from his pocket and been found by Joe Worsley who, in a moment of pure genius, had substituted the name Joe Worsley with that of Brian Ashton in Pete's contacts list. Just to make things clear, from that moment on any messages sent from Joe's phone would arrive on Pete's under the name of 'Brian Ashton'. As we sat enjoying the sunshine, anticipating the arrival of some fine French cuisine, there was an audible 'ping'. Pete had a text. As he read it, it was clear he was moving towards a state of shock. Meanwhile Joe had kicked us under the table and given a knowing wink.

'Shit, I've just had a text from Brian. Andy Gomarsall's gone down with food poisoning and it looks as though I'm in the team for Saturday. He wants to meet me in the team room in an hour. What the f*** am I going to do?'

Cottoning on to what was occurring I said, 'Well, the one thing you're not going to do is make the meeting because we're two hours away from the hotel. Why don't you send a text telling Brian that your mum and dad have taken you out for lunch and could you meet at 6.00 p.m.?' Pete decided this was a brilliant idea, even adding how delighted his parents were with the news of his selection. His response was delivered silently to Joe's phone.

Joe calmly waited for about twenty minutes before disappearing to the gents in order to compose his next communication. Several minutes after his return he hit the send button. Another 'ping' and Pete read his new message from Brian. 'Okay, thanks Pete, I'm just going to consult with Phil Vickery and Lawrence Dallaglio and will get back to you.' The fact that Brian was supposedly going to discuss the issue with myself as senior pro and Phil as captain would not have surprised Pete.

He looked across at me and with deadly seriousness said, 'Brian's going to ring you in a minute to discuss the scrum-half position. Push my case, tell him I'm the man. Do me a favour, Lol, tell him I can get more out of the forwards than any other scrum-half in England. Just convince him, Lol, convince him.'

How I didn't piss myself with laughter I'll never know, but I managed to play a straight bat and told him I would give my honest opinion to any question Brian asked me.

The rest of us continued to enjoy the meal, the company and beautiful surroundings as Pete agonised over his immediate international future. Another twenty minutes passed and the familiar sound of a new message arriving was heard. Once again it was from Brian Ashton. 'Don't worry Pete. I've just bumped into Shaun Perry and decided he'll offer us more options against Australia. Enjoy your lunch and see you tomorrow.'

Under normal circumstances Pete would have smelled a rat, but the way things had been going on the selection front, what was going on was hardly out of the ordinary. 'Give me the keys, Lol,' he said. 'I'm going to drive back and see Brian. I need to convince him. It's the quarter-final of the World Cup, for f**** sake.'

'You're not having the keys, Pete. Firstly you're not insured to drive, and more importantly my lobster is just about to arrive along with another bottle of perfectly chilled rosé.' We convinced Pete there was nothing he could do so he might as well enjoy the rest of the day.

A friend of Dan Luger's arrived a little later and asked if we wanted to go to a party at Brigitte Bardot's house along the coast. Needless to say, this received a very positive response. Pete was obviously no longer in the team so there really was very lIttle holding us back.

We arrived at the house and bizarrely (for us) the party was being held for the Australians. Past players such as Jason Little, Tim Horan and Phil Kearns were there with their partners and I also noticed the wives of several current players, including scrum-half George Gregan and flanker Phil Waugh. You can imagine the 'banter' was fairly intense. A few English players who'd been battered 36–0 by South Africa turn up at a party for Australians. I forget how many times I was asked if they could have my tickets since I wouldn't need them; were we now officially on holiday; was anyone going to turn up to play Australia on Saturday or were we just going to award them a bye to the next round to save everyone bother? It was all good-humoured stuff.

After a couple of hours at the party I decided to take control and told the lads we would be leaving shortly for Marseille and the wonders of the Holiday Inn. As we left, the Aussies wished us a safe trip and pleaded with us to put out a team on the Saturday because they had money on Australia scoring more against us than South Africa. I think it's fair to say they were feeling confident.

As the car pulled away we told Pete about our bit of fun. Let's just say he was not overly amused and after his initial use of words I couldn't possible put into print, he didn't say another thing all the way back. I suppose I couldn't blame him, but it was how the team operated, there were always wind-ups and banter going on. By the time the quarter-final on the following Saturday came round he was back to his old self.

Pete did in fact make it on to the pitch for the match, as a blood replacement for Andy Gomarsall. He may have only seen five minutes of action but by all accounts he used his time well with a classic line directed in George Gregan's direction as the Australian scrum-half prepared to put the ball in at Pete's first scrum. 'Your wife looked bloody gorgeous at Brigitte Bardot's house in St Tropez on Tuesday night. I had no idea Tim Horan and her were such good friends.' Priceless. It was sledging at its absolute best because there was a grain of truth in it. Pete had seen George's wife on Tuesday, with Tim Horan, just not in the manner in which he was insinuating. Apparently George didn't react too much, but I suspect there was much mulling over in his brain. Tuesday night, St Tropez, a party, my wife, Tim Horan ... Whatever effect Pete's words may have had, one thing is certain. We won the last twenty minutes of the match and emerged victorious 12–10 with a place in the semi-final.

Our surprise opponents turned out to be France. I say 'surprise' only because the All Blacks were such red-hot favourites that the magnificent French second-half comeback in their quarter-final encounter had shocked many. I can't say we were disappointed with the result mind you. There is no question the French were a great team, but since the days of our combative and talkative hooker Brian Moore they had always been relatively easy to rattle. A few choice words from the more vocal members of the England side, coupled with the French supporters who have a knack of turning on their team if things do not go according to plan (a second-minute Josh Lewsey try certainly knocked the wind out of their sails), and victory was ours 14–9. Another World Cup final beckoned.

The final against South Africa proved to be a match of 'what ifs' for us. What if the 'try' early in the second half by Mark Cueto had been allowed to stand? What if golden child Jonny Wilkinson had managed a better day with the boot? But the thing is, I don't deal in 'what ifs'. We lost fair and square and England had another four years to wait before hopefully putting things right. Sadly without me.

Photo Opportunities

Lee Mears

'Lee is just the type of player you want in your team, a lively character both on and off the pitch who never appears to have a down moment. His glass is always half full. Born in Torquay, he joined the Bath academy in 1997 and has never looked back. With international hookers such as Andy Long, Mark Regan and Jonathan Humphreys at Bath, it has not been an easy ride for him, but whenever he was dropped he continued to train hard in the knowledge that his chance would come again.

'This attitude earned him thirty-five England caps and although he is currently off the international scene it would not surprise me if he made a comeback in the next twelve months. Lee was also a member of the 2009 Lions tour to South Africa

and played in one Test match. I am reliably informed he is one of the players in the professional era who spends more time than most working with the community department at Bath Rugby, passing on his knowledge and enthusiasm to schools and clubs in the region. Quality.'

The World Cup is the ultimate competition for an international rugby player. Sure, a British and Irish Lions tour pushes it close, but by definition it only includes the Home Nations every four years and one of either Australia, New Zealand and South Africa every twelve years. With a World Cup all the top nations participate, with the majority of teams having to navigate an extensive qualification process in order to compete. As a result, only the very best reach the final stage of the tournament.

I made my international debut in 2005 and from that moment I was hoping to make the squad for the 2007 World Cup. Memories and images of 2003 were fresh in my mind and I knew I wanted to be a part of a similar, and equally successful, campaign. Months and months of hard preparation precede the tournament in an attempt to ensure peak fitness is achieved by each squad member. As the tournament approached we all received extensive instruction in physiological training and mental preparation as collectively we strove towards perfection (an impossible goal but always worth aiming for). It was everything I'd expected and it seemed as though nothing had been left to chance in our bid to defend the Webb Ellis Cup.

From the moment we stepped off the plane in Paris it was evident the big event was well and truly under way as masses of beret-wearing Frenchmen and women welcomed us with loads of free stuff. Thank you very much, we all thought, with arms outstretched, ready to be filled, even though Nike had already delivered a mountain of kit to every player. Even in the professional era it's still exciting to receive freebies, or stash as the boys call it. We boarded a luxury bus and were driven to a beautiful hotel next to the Palace of Versailles where we had a few photos taken for sponsors and corporate partners. Things could not have been better, our preparation was excellent and the facilities in France superb.

On the first morning I made my way to breakfast and noticed a few of the lads gathered around one of the tables looking at the back page of France's oldest newspaper *Le Figaro*. I assumed it was an article about our arrival, 'Defending Champions Prepared for Battle' or something similar. I joined the group and even with my limited French I could understand the headline, 'L'Angleterre s'ennuie déjà ('England are Bored Already'). Beneath it was a photo of Jonny Wilkinson on the steps leading from the plane, and next to him was our hooker, Mark 'Ronnie' Regan, halfway through a yawn so big most of his head had disappeared. His mum would not have been pleased. He had made no attempt to cover his mouth. It's fair to say that since landing his winning dropped goal in 2003 Jonny has become hot property, and if you're standing close to hot property in a public situation there's a good chance you're going to be photographed. It was not Ronnie's finest hour and nor was it the ideal start to our campaign. From that moment things seemed to start going against us.

Our opening match was a hard-fought 28–10 victory against

the USA. The scoreline suggests a relatively comfortable win, but the reality was a poor English performance against a skilful and battling display by the Americans. Next up were the South Africans. Yes, the match we try to forget. We were completely outplayed in a 36–0 mauling which left me finding it hard to come to terms with the fact that our preparation had been so magnificent and yet within a couple of weeks everything was turning to rat shit. We stumbled on through the group stages and then secured a decent victory over Australia in the quarter-final. Although the victory gave the team a degree of confidence, it was clear things still were not right. The overall organisation and structure was not as it should have been. This is best illustrated by a comment from one of the former England captains in the squad, Martin Corry. 'Cozza' is a stand-up guy, with a good sense of humour and is a passionate Englishman, extremely focused on his rugby. I was heading back to my room one afternoon when I saw him walking along the corridor towards me.

'Okay, Cozza?'

'Fine, Mearsy,' he replied, 'although I do feel as though I'm a member of a pub side that's just found itself in the semi-final of the World Cup.'

I can't say I entirely agreed with him, but I knew exactly what he meant.

By hook or by crook we reached the final, where once again we came unstuck against South Africa, although our performance was much better than it had been just over a month earlier. Had the Mark Cueto 'try' been given early in the second half who knows, things might have been different. You can never be satisfied with defeat, but if someone had offered me a place in the final after our group matches I would have gladly taken it.

We flew back to London and as we disembarked from the plane there was a throng of supporters to welcome us home. I think we'd shocked a lot of people by reaching the final and they wanted to show their appreciation. Obviously the numbers didn't compare to 2003, but as a squad we were pleasantly surprised and determined to act in a manner appropriate to the occasion. We may not have been conquering heroes, but we were dignified runners-up and there was no better exemplar of this than my Bath team-mate Matt Stevens, who reached the bottom of the steps down from the plane with his chest puffed out, standing proud. Until, that is, Olly Barkley grabbed his trousers and yanked them down to his ankles. Luckily Matt was wearing a pair of boxers, which was by no means a certainty. His smartest Calvin Kleins, if I remember correctly. If you ever run into Matt you can check – a photograph of the incident acts as the screen-saver on his laptop.

Did our two arrivals sum up our World Cup? I think so. We started sluggishly, woke up a bit as the tournament progressed, began to look the part, but ended up being debagged by those big South African boys.

Strange Bedfellows

Andy Gomarsall

‘Apart from goal-kickers, there are a relatively small percentage of international rugby players who score more points than the number of times they represent their country. Andy managed to achieve this feat, scoring thirty-seven points from thirty-five Test matches.

‘From an early age Andy displayed his talent as a scrum-half, leading the England Schools Under-18 team in 1992 to their first Grand Slam in eleven years. One year later he signed for my club Wasps and within a couple of seasons was knocking on the door of the England team. Although he made his international debut in 1996 I have a recollection of him being called up as a replacement for England during their World Cup campaign in 1995 aged

just twenty-one. After several seasons with Wasps it looked as though he was on a personal mission to play for as many clubs as possible during the remainder of his career, representing, Bath, Bedford, Gloucester, Worcester, Harlequins and Leeds to name a few.

'He always maintained a standard of high performance and in my opinion was one of the stand-out players during the 2007 World Cup in France. Unfortunately he was plagued by injury during his last few seasons in the game.'

Had we lost our quarter-final match against Australia in Marseille during the 2007 World Cup this story would never have seen the light of day. It would have remained a secret to which only my father and I would be privy.

My dad, Jack, supported me throughout my career and never missed any of the major matches. This was some achievement as he hates flying with a passion. Obviously if I was playing in Paris this was not a problem as he could catch the Eurostar, similarly with matches in Dublin, which for him was no more than a ferry ride and the hire of a car. However, when I was selected for the 2003 World Cup in Australia it posed a massive dilemma for him: was his desire to watch me play for my country in a World Cup greater than his fear of flying? (I still think it's odd for people to have a fear of flying; presumably they have a greater fear of crashing.) I'm not sure if he was hypnotised or suitably dosed with drugs but he made the trip and witnessed the entire event, which was surely made worthwhile when Johnno hoisted the trophy late in the evening on 22 November. Completing the return leg did nothing to alleviate his fears, so he continued wherever possible to travel by any other means than aeroplanes to watch me play my rugby.

In 2007 after a 36–0 demolition by South Africa in the pool stage, not many people expected us to make the quarter-finals of the tournament, and that included my dad. Yet with fairly unconvincing wins against USA, Samoa and Tonga we somehow managed to limp into the knockout stage with a match against Australia in Marseille. Dad and I exchanged a few phone calls and made plans for him to make the trip to the South of France, driving the entire way there himself. He packed a few things into his suitcase, threw it into the boot of the car and set off from his home in Bury St Edmunds. According to the online route planner I'd looked at it was a trip of 830 miles (providing you don't get lost).

I gave him a ring every two or three hours to check on his progress and it became apparent it wasn't proving to be a trouble-free trip. He was severely delayed near Paris travelling around the Boulevard Périphérique, one of the busiest highways in Europe, in addition to normal delays for road works and traffic accidents. After twelve hours of driving he was still many miles away. Eventually he rang to say he'd arrived, but wasn't going to be able to see me because the only hotel with vacancies was another hour's drive from Marseille. He had already made a Herculean effort to watch me play the following day and I couldn't bear the thought of him driving any further, spending the night on his own miles from the action. So I told him to make his way to the

Holiday Inn where the England team were staying. 'I'll fix you up with a meal and I've got a double bed so you might as well stay with me in my room tonight.'

I think Lawrence has covered the state of this hotel in more than enough detail so I will only pass on one additional memory of the carnage left by the Georgians. I remember walking into reception and seeing piles of what looked like sawdust dotted around. I asked the concierge what it was for. 'Sawdust?' he said. 'It was furniture last night! And now it is being used to soak up vomit.' Enough said.

Anyway my dad arrived at the hotel looking absolutely shattered. Clearly he couldn't have driven for another hour. I took him to the restaurant, ordered some food and a glass of red wine knowing it wasn't going to be long before he crashed out for the night. Twenty minutes later we were both in my bedroom, dad stripped down to his underpants and tucked up in bed. It was slightly unnerving at thirty-four years of age knowing I was about to get into the same bed as my dad, thirty years after the last time I'd had the experience.

So a few minutes later after cleaning my teeth, on the eve of the biggest game of my life up to that point, the quarter-final of a World Cup, I climbed into bed alongside my old man. Shortly after I'd dropped off to sleep I was awoken by a Canadian lumberjack, using a chainsaw to level all the trees growing in my room. That's not strictly true, but the noise of Dad snoring was at least on a par with that which accompanies the Rocky Mountain macho men. He was producing an unbelievable volume. I gave him a nudge, followed by a shove, neither of which had any effect. So I punched him on the shoulder. This caused him to wake and ask if everything was okay. I told him his snoring was so loud it was preventing me from sleeping. We then proceeded to have a husband and wife 'discussion'.

'No I'm not,' was his opening gambit.

'Yes you are,' I came back, cleverly. 'Believe me, I wouldn't make it up.'

He was becoming defensive. 'I only snore if I've had a drink, and you can't classify one glass of wine as having a drink.'

He may have been my dad but given the circumstances I had no problem replying, 'You f****** are. Now f****** shut up!'

He was still protesting his innocence as he dropped off once again. I took the opportunity of a few moments' silence to try and get back to sleep myself. An hour or so later and I was awoken again with the non-rhythmic sound of his incessant snoring. I gave him another big shove and this time, still asleep, he turned over and put his arm around me. My father. In my bed. In effect, cuddling me. And snoring. I love this man, I thought to myself, but I may need to kill him. The long night continued with me waking Dad on a regular basis and snatching brief moments of sleep during the occasional silence.

He has always been an early riser and at 6.00 a.m. I awoke to the sound of him whistling in the bathroom as he cleaned his undercarriage. Why would anyone leave the bathroom door open while completing their ablutions? I lay in bed having had a terrible night thinking how badly prepared I was for the match of my life. He came out of the bathroom, dressed, and went down to have breakfast with the England team, leaving me to try and get a few extra winks of sleep, probably doubling my total for the night.

I remember getting out of bed, showering and drawing back the curtains to see bright blue sky. We'd been informed the forecast was for rain and at that stage, with our confidence at best fragile, we believed that our best opportunity of beating Australia was in the wet. We required something to level things up a bit. This was not going to be my day, or indeed England's, I wearily told myself. Several hours later, however, our forwards had crushed the Australians in every scrum and when the referee, Alain Rolland, blew his whistle for the final time we'd thrashed them 12–10, causing the upset of the tournament.

I appreciate everything my dad's done for me over the years and all his support. However, I can honestly say we will never be sleeping in the same bed or possibly the same county again.

Purely as a matter of interest I wonder if David Beckham or any of the other football stars have shared a bed with their dad the night before a World Cup game. I think the reality is I am, and will remain, in a small club of one when it comes to this particular scenario.

Epilogue

2011

In the space of just twenty years the Rugby World Cup has grown beyond even the wildest of expectations. As I mentioned at the beginning of this book, in 1987 the tournament was watched by a worldwide television audience of 300 million. The total match attendance was 600,000 and it generated a commercial surplus of around £1 million.

Four years later and the TV audience had grown to 1.75 billion, with match attendances rising to 1 million. Commercially the figures proved the World Cup was here to stay as income of pushing £27 million generated profits in excess of £4 million. Fast forward to 2007 and you are talking profits of over £120 million with the number of spectators and viewers both more than doubling from the 1991 figures. With the television rights presold for the 2011 and 2015 tournaments it looks as though the growth will continue, although perhaps not as sharply.

Having read all the stories contributed to this book I think it's fair to say the first World Cup was an amateur affair. It was hastily organised, with the majority of competing teams treating it as little more than an end-of-season tour. Then as each subsequent tournament came around the stories indicate there was less and less drinking of alcohol, with a greater emphasis on preparation and training. (Although I am glad to say the occasional night out was still allowed by the more liberal coaches and insisted upon by players from the 'old school'.)

I just hope as rugby continues to spread around the globe, with ever more countries participating, the essence of the game is not lost. Obviously, wherever it's played professionally the players have a responsibility as they are effectively representing a business and being paid for their services. However, there must be enjoyment in what they do, and surely the opportunity to let off a bit of steam can still be built into their training and development programmes. I know from my time with Wasps, England and the Lions, a good piss-up with the boys did as much to engender team spirit and bonding as any official exercise purporting to achieve the same results. I shudder when I think of a certain 'team-building weekend with the marines'!

I've done both, and benefited from both, and believe each has its place in the preparation of teams even at the highest level. To be honest, whenever I meet up with former team-mates and people I've been on tour with the conversation is always about a particular get together, or some ridiculous antics someone got up to. I can't recall conversations about specific training sessions or team meetings, no matter how inspirational they may have been. I suppose what I want is for the modern-day player to continue to get as much fun from the game as I did, to work hard and also, from time to time, play hard.

As for the 2011 Rugby World Cup, this book will be finished

before a ball is kicked, so I will make my prediction now, which will prevent me from changing my mind after the first round of pool games. I am a proud Englishman who will always support my country in everything they do. However, I do not see them winning this time around. They've taken giant strides in the right direction over the last eighteen months but probably not quite far enough. I feel a semi-final will be a good result, and expect nothing less than a quarter-final spot. As for the winners, it's difficult to see past New Zealand, particularly as they are on home soil. Many of us have joked how they always manage to peak between tournaments and then fall short when it matters. I know they were devastated to lose against France in their quarter-final four years ago, and it feels as though they've been building towards this World Cup ever since.

Australia and South Africa will also progress deep into the tournament and I anticipate one of these two teams will be contesting the final. Looking at other nations, the French have the ability to reach the final if they play to their potential, as do Argentina, but ultimately I think it will come down to the Wallabies or the Springboks to take on the All Blacks.

There we go, I've stuck my neck out and plumped for New Zealand to win, but as we all know the beauty of sport is its unpredictability. Nothing would give me more pleasure than being proved wrong. I'll be cheering louder than anyone if England lift the Webb Ellis Cup on Sunday 23 October in Auckland.

Bring it on.

Acknowledgements

Once again, although my name appears on the cover, this book could not have happened without the help, hard work and support of many people.

First and foremost I would like to thank all the players who have contributed stories and anecdotes. Thank you guys. I know everyone at Wooden Spoon very much appreciates the time and effort you put into this project. There would be 300 blank pages here if it wasn't for you. Not the best of reading material, although I am pretty sure some of the boys I played with over the years would have still found it quite challenging. 'Why aren't there any chapters, Lol?' I can hear them say. So thank you once again, all of you, for turning those empty pages into an entertaining and often informative read.

I would also like to thank the players and coaches that I have worked with and played against. Without the rugby community, there would be no stories for anyone to tell. Thank you. It has been a hell of a lot of fun.

A special thanks to David Trick who is one of life's great characters. He has worked incredibly hard and helped me produce the book I wanted. Thanks also to my business manager Richard Relton for keeping me and everything else on track.

The book could not have happened without my publishers, Simon & Schuster. My thanks to the team for helping me pull this off again and for your patience, understanding and professionalism in producing a book I am delighted with. It got a bit tight I know. In particular I would like to thank Rhea Halford for all her hard work, Kerr MacRae for helping kick start the whole thing and Anna Robinson for being the best publicist you could ever want.

A special mention to David Wilson who once more worked round the clock to make sense of our words and turn them into a book to be proud of.

Thanks also to John Griffiths for keeping me right on my facts. I am grateful for the work you undertook to check everything for me. If any additional screw ups have crept in, they are entirely my fault.

Of course the people who deserve the greatest thanks are my family. Dad, Alice, Ella, Josie and Enzo. I am very lucky to have you.

Finally, thanks to you, the reader, for buying this book and supporting Wooden Spoon. I hope you have as much fun reading it as I have had in pulling it all together.

Thank you all.

Wooden Spoon

The children's charity of rugby

Dear Reader,

Thanks to the kindness of Lawrence Dallaglio, Wooden Spoon has been chosen as the charity to benefit from the sales of this book, we are extremely grateful for all the support that Lawrence has given Spoon over the years.

Wooden Spoon is a children's charity founded in 1983 and exists to make a positive impact on the lives of disadvantaged children and young people through our commitment to quality charitable work.

We partner with the rugby community, receiving their invaluable support for our activities and the opportunity to raise awareness of the work we do. We organise our own fundraising events and initiatives, raise the money and donate as much as we can to help mentally, physically or socially disadvantaged children and young people.

Over the years, we have donated over £16m and have diversified from purely capital projects such as medical treatment and recovery centres, sports and activity areas, sensory rooms and gardens to include outreach programmes that tackle youth crime and unemployment.

Why not join us... visit **www.woodenspoon.com**

Yours sincerely

Bill Hill
Chief Executive

Find us on FaceBook: **www.facebook.com/SpoonyWS** *or*
Twitter: **@charityspoon**

www.woodenspoon.com
Royal Patron: HRH The Princess Royal
Rugby Patrons: Rugby Football Union Scottish Rugby Union Welsh Rugby Union Irish Rugby Football Union Rugby Football League
Postal Address: 41 Frimley High Street, Frimley, Surrey GU16 7HJ
Tel: 01276 410180 Fax: 01276 410181 Email: charity@woodenspoon.com
The Wooden Spoon Society is a company Limited by Guarantee. Reg Office Address: 1st Floor, Pellipar House, 9 Cloak Lane, London, EC4R 2RU.
Company Reg No: 1847860.The Wooden Spoon Society is a registered charity in England and Wales (Reg No: 326691) and in Scotland (Reg No: SC039247)